River of
GRACE

"If, like me, you have experienced failure or loss and can't quite find your way out of the darkness, you will appreciate this book. Susan Bailey offers gentle reflections with graceful tools that bring light, creative renewal, and a fuller Christian life."

Rev. Robert Reed
President of CatholicTV and author of *Renewed*

"Susan Bailey's powerful and beautifully written book is much more than an insightful spiritual memoir. *River of Grace* is also a brilliant reflection on the connections between creativity and grace."

Amy Belding Brown
Author of *Flight of the Sparrow*

"In this gentle book, Susan Bailey reminds us that every experience is awash in blessing. All we need to do is navigate the river of grace that flows through it to discover the meaning and possibility it offers."

Sr. Bridget Haase, O.S.U.
Cohost of *Spirit and Life*

"Susan Bailey's personal stories and her try-this-yourself suggestions remind readers to be gentle and patient with themselves in the aftermath of grief or loss. True healing may be less a renewal of the old self and more a re-creation of someone new."

Pat Gohn
Author of *Blessed, Beautiful, and Bodacious*

"Susan Bailey not only invites the reader into stories, but also into experience. Through simple practices, ordinary materials, and here-and-now situations, she provides moments in which we can understand the workings of the Spirit and connect with God's ongoing 'flow' of grace in us."

Vinita Hampton Wright
Catholic blogger and author of *The Art of Spiritual Writing*

River of GRACE

Creative Passages Through Difficult Times

SUSAN BAILEY

AVE MARIA PRESS AVE Notre Dame, Indiana

Founded in 1865, Ave Maria Press is a ministry of the United States Province of Holy Cross.

www.avemariapress.com

Paperback: ISBN-13 978-1-59471-572-3

E-book: ISBN-13 978-1-59471-573-0

Cover image © FogStock LLC / FogStock LLC.

Cover and text design by Christopher D. Tobin.

Printed and bound in the United States of America.

Library of Congress Cataloging-in-Publication Data
Bailey, Susan (Professional Musician)
    River of grace : creative passages through difficult times / Susan Bailey.
        pages cm
    Includes bibliographical references.
    ISBN 978-1-59471-572-3 -- ISBN 1-59471-572-6
1. Christian life--Catholic authors. 2. Spiritual life--Catholic Church. 3. Loss (Psychology)--Religious aspects--Catholic Church. 4. Suffering--Religious aspects--Catholic Church. I. Title.
    BX2350.3.B334 2015
    248.4'82--dc23
                            2015017556

With all of my heart I dedicate this book to my parents,
Deb and Herb Hoyle, who left me legacies of faith,
music, reading and writing, curiosity, a love of learning and
the outdoors, and most of all, lasting examples of kindness,
thoughtfulness, selfless giving, and compassion.

Contents

Contents

Introduction

Navigating through Life in the River of Grace

> Wherever the river goes, every living creature that swarms
> will live, and there will be very many fish, once these
> waters reach there. It will become fresh; and everything
> will live where the river goes. . . . On the banks, on both
> sides of the river, there will grow all kinds of trees for
> food. Their leaves will not wither nor their fruit fail, but
> they will bear fresh fruit every month, because the water
> for them flows from the sanctuary. Their fruit will be for
> food, and their leaves for healing.
>
> —Ezekiel 47:9, 12

I love the sound of water. Rushing. Lapping. Dripping. So does
my husband. We have two small fountains on our deck just
so we can hear that lapping sound. At night along with the
crickets and locusts, we can hear the water gurgling in a rhythmic
flow. Water has always been important to me in all its forms:
bath, pool, pond, river, ocean.

Water has taught me many things. I've learned about trust
by allowing the current to carry me. It has cultivated a shared
harmony between my husband and me. It's shown me that I
can ride the rapids and emerge shaken but standing. For those
who pay attention to water, it offers a continual flow of lessons.

My appreciation of the gift and lessons of water began years ago, during a season of losses. That was when my husband suggested we purchase a kayak. Our then new home was in a region of many rivers and ponds, including a boat landing just five minutes from our house. We tested canoes and kayaks, and the minute I sank into the seat of the kayak I knew this was where I belonged. It put me as close to the water as I could get. I could run my hands through it and even dip my toes. My husband and I bought a tandem kayak, and it changed our lives.

It's interesting how something so ordinary can reveal such profound spiritual lessons. In our trips together I noticed the increased harmony between us. I was aware of being filled with deep peace that would linger long after the trip. The quiet allowed me to take in what was around me, most especially how the current carried us to new and wonderful places. I began to equate that current of the river with God's grace. Sometimes we would let the flow do the work for us, especially if we needed a rest from paddling. But we could also work *with* the current *through* our synchronized paddling to arrive sooner at the agreed destination. Along the way I could take in the sights, smells, and sensations of splashing water, warm breezes, and the greenery and sweet fragrances of the summer season, all of which filled me with a sense of well-being. These tactile experiences provided a powerful metaphor, demonstrating that the current of God's grace promised the same thing for my life if I but worked in partnership with him, trusted that I would be carried, and believed that I was meant to be brought to a better place. Kayaking taught me to look for and appreciate the smallest of details in God's creation: the color of the water, the flowers along the shore, the curve of the branches of a tree, the great blue heron standing in majestic splendor. If all I cared about was getting to my final destination, I would miss out on the best part, which was the journey itself. The message became clear: if I don't plant myself in the present moment, remaining alert to all of those lessons and small blessings God provides along the way, I will miss much of what he intends to give me. I came to discover that those small blessings were in abundance and would continue to multiply, not only when the journey was easy, but also when it became difficult and frightening. The river of grace is in constant motion, and only when I submit to that motion will I discover the many blessings that lie in the present moment. The longer I am in the river, the richer my life becomes.

In the last ten years I have known great losses, some expected, some not. Each loss, however, seemed to create a new inlet to the river. The river, after all, is not a straight line. New tributaries open, each with a strong current beckoning me into a new adventure. One of the first lessons of the river was in seeing obedience to God not as onerous "do nots" but as exhilarating "dos"! As I learned to be carried by grace, I began to sense invitations to a better way of being. As my trust grew, I allowed God to take me into those tricky currents, trying things that once seemed "crazy" and "foolish." The more I allowed myself to be carried, the more I learned how to say yes to life. As a result, my faith grew stronger, my joy and gratitude deeper. For the first time in my life, I learned how to dream.

The flow of the river of grace is not always peaceful; it takes trust to hang on when the whitewater moments hit. In the last ten years I have been carried off by the rapids, slammed into rocks, and plummeted over waterfalls; I came out bloodied and chastened, yet wiser and stronger. Embedded in those struggles is the belief that God would provide resting places along the shore and docks to offload my burdens. The difficult passages became the means of a loving Father to mold, shape, and transform me; they taught me that I am indeed a beloved daughter of God.

These stories are also about understanding the nature of the current and letting the river of grace fill and change me. When we face losses, we are given a different kind of clarity. As a result, I have learned to leave a good portion of my life behind, separating from people and parts of myself I once thought vital to my being. I've discovered joy for the first time even in the midst of sorrow. And an exhilarating rebirth of creativity has taken place. I've lost much, but gained so much in the process. Gratitude is replacing bitterness; it is fueling that joy.

This concept of a continuous, living flow of grace is new to me despite being raised Catholic. Although faith had been important to me as a child growing up in the Church, it dried up during my twenties and thirties. I filled the emptiness with ambition, throwing my energy into pursuing a career. I became self-absorbed, sullen, and frustrated. My faith dissolved into a quagmire of doubts except for one saving grace: a persistent gut feeling that the Eucharist was special. That vague yet strong feeling kept me going to Mass during those years until a conversion experience in my late thirties brought me back home to a living, breathing faith.

The seeds of faith were planted during my childhood. In those days the Mass was said in Latin and I did not understand a word of it. Yet when I received Communion I found myself thinking of concrete images that reinforced in my mind and heart that this wafer was special, even if it did taste like cardboard. I'd picture the foyer of my house with its hardwood floor scrubbed clean and made shiny. Or I'd imagine a rosebush growing in my heart. Those images represented a child's understanding of being made clean when we go to Mass (the clean and shiny floor) and that something beautiful grows within us when we receive the Body of Christ (as in the rosebush).

Imaginings of everyday material things planted a love of the Eucharist within me that gave me something to hold on to during my crisis of faith. It was a foreshadowing of how kayaking on the river would provide the concrete metaphor for God's grace. The physical things of this world—water and rivers, wafers, chalices filled with wine, shiny floors and growing rosebushes—are provided by God as a starting point, guiding us into the mystery and transformation of the spiritual life.

April 22, 2010, not only marked the day I lost my mother; it was also the day I began to find my authentic self. It started with a series of simple yeses on the river of grace:

- Yes to being an orphan as both of my parents were gone.

- Yes to accepting another sort of death, the loss of my singing voice and service to the Church as a cantor.

- Yes to saying good-bye to my old life as a professional musician.

- Yes to visiting a homebound woman each week to bring her Communion just two weeks after losing my mother.

- Yes to immersing myself in an old love, the life and works of Louisa May Alcott, and to blogging and engaging in new communities.

- Yes to teaching high school CCD even though I was terrified of teenagers.

- Yes to accepting, eventually, my new vocation from God as a writer.

It was loss that immersed me into the watery flow of God's spirit and led me downstream. It was loss that drenched me in grace and blessings, which multiplied with each subsequent yes. Obedience changed from that oppressive no to a freeing yes, leading to growth, acceptance, and new adventures, to a transformation of loss.

This book shares the lessons of the journey, the passage from grief to joy, from confusion to insight, and from bitterness to deep gratitude. It is also a book that provides help: "Flow Lessons"—practical and creative ways to review the process, plus navigational tools for those white-water times. There are additional resources on my website, beasone.org; click on the tab "Flow Lessons." All of the Flow Lessons include prayerful exercises that will take spiritual concepts and relate them to something concrete in our everyday lives in order to facilitate greater understanding. If we think of the wafer as being the material form of the Eucharist, as something we can see, touch, and eat, we can have a starting point for contemplating its deep spiritual mystery. You will have an opportunity to test drive such an exercise at the end of this preface.

We are surrounded with such tactile examples in our own churches and within the Mass, whether it be the beautiful art that adorns the walls and windows, the priestly vestments and their symbolic colors signaling a particular liturgical season, the aroma of incense, the sounds of music, the handshakes, hugs, and kisses exchanged during the Sign of Peace, or the taste and texture of the bread and wine. These and more act as guides— entry points into spiritual mysteries. My hope is that you can experience your own epiphanies of God's grace, as I did from my childhood memories of the Eucharist and kayaking on the river.

While there are numerous books dealing with grief, its stages and process, this one presents a new dimension with its promise of creative transformation, something that is meant for all of us. The story of a journey of losses may also be a story that puts a kayak on the river as a first step toward the discovery and realization of the creative life. Acknowledging the creativity within us is a form of spiritual awakening as we take things that already exist and make something new from them.

The artistic life is fraught with land mines of the ego, self-absorption, and the emotions. It requires solitude, creating a delicate balancing act especially for women who are wives and mothers. Creative women I know have found it difficult to fully embrace their vocations as artists, whether it is in art, music, writing, and so on, because of the false notion that it is "selfish" to indulge in self-expression. By placing our creativity into God's care and trusting his vision as each loss unfolds, we become free to express the creative vocation for his service, becoming true to ourselves in the process.

Many of us believe we have no capacity for creativity because we lack talent in the fine arts. Although I do have some of that talent, I believe it to be merely a tool for the more basic purpose of creating something new by combining elements that already exist. The Holy Spirit is the example, hovering over the waters, as depicted in Genesis, in preparation for the creation of the world. The Spirit of God used the formless earth to create light, sky, land, vegetation, and animals. He drew from the existing dust to create man; woman was created from a rib inside of the man. Something new was created from what already existed. We are called to do the same in every little action in our lives. I hope to show through this book how each of us can discover that creativity that God has planted within us.

Consider this book as shared spiritual lessons and wisdom, where a friend shares with another friend how her faith got her through tough times and had her life transformed in amazing ways. I am a big believer in being part of a community where we encourage and help others. By sharing pieces of my story, I hope that you will discover a place, a haven, to enter in where you can explore your own stories and processes. Faith-sharing among friends helps to provide that safe haven.

Beginning with the metaphor of a river as the means by which one is guided and immersed in the spiritual life, I share spiritual lessons learned from the various losses I experienced and the transformation that resulted from my consenting to travel down that river of grace. My hope is that your experience in the "river" is transformative, informative, and Spirit filled, despite—and sometimes because of—the white waters.

Flow Lesson 1

Digesting the Eucharist

Materials needed: pen or pencil and paper, food, your imagination

Pick a quiet place in your home to do this exercise, and make sure you can sit still comfortably for several minutes. To begin, take a moment to be still with God. If you are having trouble with noise in your mind from the cares of the day, close your eyes and imagine a tree in winter filled with screeching birds. The tree is dense with these birds, and the noise is unbearable. Now watch as each bird flies away. Attach a thought or care to that flying bird and bid it adieu. Do this until the tree is entirely empty of birds and it is quiet.

After a few moments of quiet, go to the kitchen and fix yourself something to eat that is both nutritious and something you really like. As you prepare your food, say a prayer of thanksgiving to God for that food and for the privilege of eating it in his presence.

Return with your food to the place you designated for this exercise and examine it carefully. Write down a few descriptive phrases about the food, noting its color, smell, and texture. Now take a bite and chew slowly, thinking about how the food tastes, what it feels like in your mouth, and what you enjoy about that food. Write down phrases that pop into your mind.

When you finish your meal, think about where food goes after you eat it, how it travels to your stomach, is digested, and then is circulated throughout your body via your bloodstream. As you are thinking about that, consider how you are feeling: Do you feel energized and satisfied after eating? Does it give you what you need to carry on with your day? Write down your impressions, and then put your piece of paper in a prominent place so you will remember to take it with you the next time you go to Mass. Ask God to take what you have written and plant it on your heart for when you receive Communion.

During Mass take out that piece of paper and read it *before* you receive the Eucharist. Now consider the Eucharist in the same way you considered the food you ate during your meditation. Be mindful of the texture of the wafer as you receive it and notice how you eat it: Do you chew it or let it dissolve? Think about why you eat it in that way and how it makes you feel. If you also receive the wine, do you hold the wafer in your mouth and wait to consume it until you drink the wine? How does the wine add to the experience?

When you get back to your place, think about the wafer and the wine being digested, soon to be coursing through your veins. What symbols come to mind, if any? How will the Eucharist nourish you, both spiritually and physically? Believing that the Eucharist is the Body and Blood of Christ, how does it make you feel to know it is now present within your body? Does it increase your sense of intimacy with Jesus?

When you get home from Mass, take a few moments to write down your impressions of receiving Communion, and

compare notes. Ask God to continue to offer insight, opening
the eyes of your mind to new ideas and possibilities.

Chapter 1—Discovering the Flow of Grace

What God Taught Me through My Kayak

At first I resisted the idea of purchasing a kayak. We were in a time of loss—debt—and money was tight. But my husband, Rich, wore me down. We both loved the water, and it was a way to discover our central Massachusetts town and surrounding towns. He found a used tandem kayak (it seats two) at a good price and drove four hours to neighboring New Hampshire to pick it up. A boat landing was right down the street, and so we set sail. Right away I knew this new hobby was going to have a positive impact on our lives.

Rich and I have enjoyed a happy, lifelong relationship. We dated in high school and married just out of college. We shared the same values about life, particularly when it came to our faith, but when it got down to doing things together, we came up short. The kayak solved that problem.

From the moment we stepped into the boat, we noticed a harmony between us. Usually competitive with each other, we instead worked in partnership. We took many leisurely trips, appreciating the natural landscape on the quieter ponds while admiring all the beautiful waterfront properties on the larger lakes. Sometimes we'd talk, but often we just paddled along, enjoying our time together in silence.

I took such pleasure in kayaking that I began to daydream about it. Sitting as close to the water as I could . . . sunshine on my face . . . lush, sweet-smelling greenery . . . dragging my hands through the warm, clear water . . . splashing it on my hot feet . . . drifting downstream, letting the current carry me . . . taking time just to be . . .

My daydreams seemed to be suggesting that the concrete experience of the water contained something deeper, a metaphor, a bridge of understanding to the spiritual life: What if I allowed God to be that current that carried me? That current, I realized, was *grace*. Grace had always been there, but I had never before acknowledged it. Sometimes the flow of grace was gentle yet persistent, while at other times it swirled with great power as it carried me through difficult times over waterfalls and through chaotic whirlpools. Even when I was swept under by this river of grace, I was protected and changed.

Putting that kayak in the river in 2007 occurred at a time when peace was much needed. We had experienced turbulence over the last several years, and fear had become my constant companion. In reflecting on the peace encountered in the boat and connecting it to grace, I realized that we had also known of the power of grace during that turbulence.

Consigning the experience of the kayak to grace was not unlike the connection I had made as a child between a "clean floor" and receiving the Eucharist. Obviously something of my religious education had sunken in: intuitively I understood that attending Mass and taking Communion cleansed me of my lesser sins. In both cases my imagination helped me to associate a familiar image with a deep spiritual mystery.

Kayaking acted as a *catalyst*, opening my mind to something that God wanted to reveal to me, just as my imagining a "clean floor" prompted an innate appreciation of the Eucharist. Why did such images and memories prompt such a strong and lasting reaction?

Perhaps as you read this, there may be concrete images in your memory that prompt a strong, positive reaction. Maybe that memory provokes a sudden wave of nostalgia. Perhaps as you think it over, that image leads you further, to some kind of truth. Smells are often great catalysts (such as the scent of perfume or a flower, reminding you of incense and thus God's lingering presence). The common element that I detect in these catalysts is a *love* of something. Love of the peace and harmony that kayaking provided. Love of having a "clean floor" (meaning a life put back in order) by receiving Communion. Because thinking on these things evoked pleasant feelings, I spent time reflecting on them to relive those feelings. Somewhere along the way, that love led me to God.

Flow Lesson 2

What Is Your Spiritual Catalyst?

Materials needed: pen or pencil and paper, your memories

Take a moment to be still with God, taking several long and deep breaths and listening as you breathe. In and out, in and out. Be conscious of the rhythm of the breathing. As you breathe in, whisper the name of Jesus; as you breathe out, whisper, "Be with me." Do this for several moments until you feel quiet and still.

Next, take a piece of paper and fold it vertically in half so that you have two columns. Now recall one memory, object, or smell that makes you feel especially good. In thinking of it, what words pop into your mind? Write them down in the left-hand column. What feelings come to mind? Why do you feel that way? Write those down, too, in the same column.

Look at your list. Are there any words on that list that you could equate with your relationship with God? Can you match up any of those impressions with how you feel when you spend time with God, either in a formal setting, such as attending Mass or a worship service, or on your own, praying for yourself or others or simply meditating? In the right-hand column, write down any words that pop into your head when you think of your experience with God. Once your list is done, see if there are any similarities between the list in the left-hand column and the list in the right. If you see similarities, draw a line from the word or words in the left-hand column to the one in the right. Is there a possibility that, in the future, your favorite memory, object, or aroma could prompt a pleasant memory about attending church or simply being in the presence of God?

Do not be disturbed if you can't see an immediate connection; it can take some practice. Ask God to reveal it to you over the course of several days, and then look at your notes again to see if a connection becomes more evident.

When the Rug Is Pulled Out from Under

Just as our faith tradition is rich with common symbols that help us begin to grasp complex spiritual mysteries, so too is the world around us. It gives new meaning to Jesus' exhortation: "Truly I tell you, unless you change and become like children, you will never enter the kingdom of heaven" (Mt 18:3). Often as adults we can no longer see what children so readily do in their mind's eye. A once active imagination can be dulled by the responsibilities and burdens of everyday living; we can lose that ability to see beneath the surface and between the lines, fooled into thinking there is nothing new to discover. Creativity, like any muscle, needs to be exercised, or it begins to atrophy. The kayak was the beginning of an awakening of that eye of a child in me. Little did I know just how much God intended to stir that pot of creativity and how much that pot would reveal.

We've all heard the expression "having the rug pulled out from under you." Imagine how that would feel: there's a jolt to your body, and you are thrown into the air. And you can do nothing about it as you then come crashing down. A searing pain shoots through your body, and you cry out. For a time you can't move and you lie still, waiting for your breath to return and the pain to subside. As your mind starts to clear, you react, either by lying still and moaning in pain or by lashing out at the person who did this to you or at no one in particular. Your reaction is instinctual.

But you have a choice, then. Could relying on God's grace also be part of that instinctual response?

Back in September 2003, I received a phone call that pulled that rug out from under me. My eighty-three-year-old father, recently diagnosed with a brain tumor, had undergone a biopsy. The procedure had gone terribly wrong, causing hemorrhaging in the brain; my father was unconscious in the ICU. The tumor in his brain was diagnosed as gliobastoma: stage-four brain cancer. Due to its location, it was inoperable.

For most of us the sense that we are losing a parent produces panic. For me, the news struck with such force that I could hardly keep it together. I bent over and wailed, knowing I would soon lose him.

This was the gentle man who had guided our family with his quiet strength and selfless love. He gave me my music and taught me the value of silence and solitude. He had introduced me to the Catholic Church with all of its rich mystery that would shape my life forever. As a child I had snuggled with him in his favorite chair, listening to stories and playing finger games. He had done the same with my children. We had laughed, loved, and struggled together. Now he was dying.

My sister, brother, and I worked with our mother to provide our father with the best care we could while navigating the complex medical and financial issues. There was no time to think or to process emotions. Most of us during these times do the one thing we can do: act out of pure instinct. During that time I allowed myself to be carried by God, even though I didn't recognize it.

How do we develop that instinct to turn to God without a thought? Is there a spouse, family member, or close friend that you turn to without question when you are in need? Why do you seek out that person? Think back over the amount of time and effort invested in that relationship; hasn't it been a lot like storing away treasure, treasure that each of you can count upon when needed? You love and trust each other because you have built something that is lasting. You would help out your special person in a heartbeat, and he or she would do the same for you. Instinctually, you turn to what you can count on.

Turning to God without Question

Habits ingrained from my childhood, such as regularly attending Mass, built a strong foundation upon which I could lean. Now during this time of chaos my faith was changing at a fundamental level. I had always thought about God and said my prayers;

I read the Bible, attended Mass every Sunday, and volunteered my time. Although I had experienced moments of conversion, once as a teenager and another time in my late thirties, I had never truly given myself over to God's grace. Now I turned to him without question. Instinct told me it was the only way to get through this difficult period and be of some use to my family. For the first time, I allowed God to carry me on this river of grace.

It fascinates me now as I reflect on how I was able to perceive God even as the world was crashing in around me. A quotation from St. Faustina says it so clearly: "O Jesus, hidden God, my heart perceives You though veils hide You."[1] My heart and mind were engulfed in my father's illness, and yet, somehow, I sensed that God was there. Perhaps it was because of the constant love and support that Rich showed me during this time. Maybe it was because of my friends, keeping us all in their prayers. It could be how we as a family worked together to give my father everything he needed because we loved him. I realize now that God was revealing himself through the love being shown to me by family and friends. They were the concrete revelation, much like Holy Communion, "the mystery of God with us, hidden by veils of bread and wine."[2] Four months after being diagnosed, my father quietly passed away. Although he had been estranged from the Church, he allowed a priest to visit him and anoint him with oil. Unable to speak, he acknowledged the priest with a smile. I believed then that all the prayers offered by family and friends had been answered; my father would be all right. Rich and I had been appealing to Our Lady of Perpetual Help for her intercession; during preparations for my father's funeral, we saw what I took to be signs of affirmation: icons of Our Lady of Perpetual Help appearing in unexpected places. We found comfort in these signs. Grace had carried me through the turmoil and deposited me safely on the other side. I was broken but not defeated.

Those of you who have experienced grief know it to be mysterious, even arbitrary and confusing. The only knowledge I had of it was what I had seen portrayed on television and in the movies: crying, depression, anger, and lethargy. I experienced some of that, but mostly I just felt out of control, unable to handle even the most mundane changes in my life. One week after the family hairdresser retired, and our next-door neighbor decided to move, something snapped inside. Vowing to be an agent of change rather than its victim, I too decided it was time for our family to move.

Purchasing a house was something Rich and I never would have considered before my father died. Financial problems had plagued us throughout our marriage. Yet suddenly the condominium we had lived in for the last sixteen years felt crowded. Our two children, now teenagers, craved privacy; my husband and son were at odds with each other, and I felt closed in. We needed more space.

My new obsession with buying a house confused me; I didn't know if it was the right thing to do. I sought out our parish priest and asked for advice; he assured me that desiring a major change in my life was a normal process of grief. He also referred me to a counselor to both process the grief and understand what I was truly longing for. Working with the counselor, I discerned that it was all right to proceed.

We sold our condominium in just one day. One year after my father died, we moved into a wonderful house. I walked through the rooms in sheer amazement, thanking God over and over for this favor. I smiled thinking of how proud my father would have been of us and how much he would have loved this house. Taking this positive step for our family did a lot to mitigate my grief by putting energy into something that attended to the needs of our family.

Carried by Grace

Yes, the rug had been pulled out from under me. Yes, I landed with a crash. Clinging to God through my prayers while being strengthened and consoled by the love and prayers of my family and friends, I rode out the rough patches, finding myself in a new home and receiving healing in grace's still pool of gratitude. It was after this full experience of life carried by grace that I came to associate it with a concrete reminder: our kayak.

Such a profound concept through a simple object — it took me a long time to accept that God could work in that way. As a child, I learned that grace came through the sacraments: Baptism, Confirmation, Reconciliation, regular reception of the Eucharist, Anointing of the Sick, and Matrimony. I grew up thinking that grace came from a church building, granted by a priest during a formal gathering such as the Mass; it never occurred to me that it could come from elsewhere, especially something as mundane as a boat.

My recollection of grace was that it was administered at certain times: it was planted in me when I was baptized and sealed within me when I was confirmed. Every Sunday I received the Eucharist, which fed me for the coming week. And when I did something wrong and was separated from God's grace, I sought out the sacrament of Reconciliation, which would cleanse me and restore that connection. Grace was meant to nourish and to heal. I could not generate it, nor earn it; I could only receive it as a gift freely given by God. The Letter to the Ephesians reads: "For by grace you have been saved through faith, and this is not your own doing; it is the gift of God—not the result of works, so that no one may boast"(Eph 2:8–9). Grace is as necessary to my spiritual life as food and water are to my body. Yet I never grasped the concept that grace is *constant*; it *never* stops flowing.

How many of us have inadvertently locked God inside of our churches, separating him from everyday life experience? Scripture is clear that God is everywhere: "Where can I go from your spirit? Or where can I flee from your presence?" (Ps 139:7). How then does this presence become a continuing reality in our lives?

While I can point to the kayak as a means of illustrating the living force of grace, I cannot say for sure how or when that bridge was built that connected the abstract concept to the living reality. I literally just woke up one day and surmised it. I suppose it points again to what prompted the connection: the flow of the water resembling the flow of grace. Since I love water, I think about it a lot. Kayaking made me daydream about it. Could spending that much time in thought about water have helped me make the connection? Perhaps there was a point when I turned to God and asked him what it all meant, but I don't recall. Asking for wisdom, however, is a good start; it's a prayer request that is often answered both quickly and decisively. I get the impression that God delights in such requests. There are times when I have to keep asking for wisdom if I am being particularly dense. But once I have asked, it is my job to keep an open mind as to how the Lord will respond. It can come through a private revelation, perhaps from reading scripture. It could also come through conversing with others. Maybe the connection comes through some common experience in our daily lives, such as kayaking. God is creative in the way he answers our prayers.

In grief and loss most of us look to our mentors—those who have faced the abyss and somehow have overcome their fear or understood something ringing clear as a bell about faith or grace. Learning from them about how they went through their process helps us begin ours. I found such mentors as I began to search the scriptures. In Genesis I was struck by the intimate friendship between God and Abraham and how it was formed. I looked at what I could learn from Abraham: how he was open, honest, vulnerable, and unwavering in his trust. And I looked at what I could learn about God from this friendship: how he lavished his love and blessings upon Abraham, making this elderly and childless man the father of many nations. I began reading the gospel texts and saw Jesus caring for countless individuals, healing them of physical, emotional, and psychological wounds. My wounds. Our wounds. He wept with Martha, Mary, and their family and friends over the death of Lazarus before raising him to life again. He was moved to tears over the plight of Jerusalem. He sacrificed his life and rose again for this healing of our wounds.

Over and over again the scriptures showed me that God longs to reach out to us, to be in a personal relationship with his creatures. With a boundless and tender love, the Lord pursued Abraham. Abraham turned to God in his grief over not having a child, and God granted him his deepest desire even as all seemed lost. Then in the gospel texts, I saw Jesus healing the wounds of those around him, forming intimate friendships with men and women in his circle, and finally sacrificing his life for everyone: past, present, and future. This is what a lover does for his beloved.

Entering into such a relationship with God is challenging. We live in a world where religion is viewed with increased hostility. Many of us are tempted to go it alone because we either feel the Church has failed us, or we think we don't need it. But personal experience has demonstrated to me the impossibility of maintaining that kind of relationship with God without the support of a church community. For eighteen years of my life, alone in my doubts and confusion, I was discouraged to the point where I had almost no relationship with God. But just as the disciples gathered to sit at the feet of their master to learn, we too need to gather together for guidance. In the gospel texts I can watch the journey of the twelve apostles accompanying Jesus during his three-year mission and see the earthly and concrete example of a supportive community, one we are meant to imitate. The common bond for the disciples is their love for Jesus. This earthly example reflects the divine community present in the Holy Trinity: an endless circle of love between the Father, Son, and Holy Spirit.

As vital as it is to come to church, limiting ourselves in our thinking that God belongs only within the walls of that church can be harmful. The gospels show us that living our faith out in the world is vital to our spiritual growth and health. It is outside of those walls that we can deepen this relationship through various means:

- meditation on God's holy Word
- the reading of spiritual books
- time spent in prayer
- building friendships with other believers
- serving others

Discovering our own catalysts, those concrete earthly things that build bridges to spiritual understanding and intimacy, will enhance our life journey. I believe that God delights in helping us know him better by using his creation to discover him. The possibilities are endless, and it all begins with something you love: reading a good book, taking a walk, quilting or crocheting, drawing or painting, dancing, writing letters to family and friends, journaling, swimming, running and other kinds of sports, cooking and entertaining, creating a beautiful and loving home, socializing, solving mathematical problems, stargazing, researching, even just brainstorming or daydreaming. Any or all of these things constitute our own personal creative expression, and it is through that expression (perhaps yet to be discovered or awakened within us) that we can grow closer to the Lord. God uses those things we love to draw us from the known into the unknown and into a deeper relationship with him.

From the Known to the Unknown

Upon reflection I see that those childhood images of the "clean floor" and the rosebush in my heart were invitations from God to love him through the Eucharist. The Eucharist then became the means by which I kept returning to God each time I wandered away.

Our Creator shaped and formed us, longing to communicate with us and using various means to do that. When we acknowledge our need for God by recognizing our innate brokenness and weakness, the Lord will reveal himself in the minutest detail of our everyday experience. One of the gifts that can come through loss is an exceptional perception: we often notice things that others don't. It's as if that eye of our inner child is opened after a long sleep. And accepting those new discoveries can be a means of grace.

Somewhere along the way I learned to see God in the natural world around me. Because of this I began to attribute the harmony between Rich and myself in the kayak as coming from God. In meditating on the experience of the river, I heard the invitation from God, asking me to let him be the guiding current in my life. Obedience, as I mentioned, has been a word I had long associated with no; now it has changed to yes: yes to partnering with God in something wonderful and life-giving.

Indeed, God *could* teach me something profound through a simple kayak.

This lesson came at a most opportune time. The honeymoon period in the new house lasted about a year before being undone by an old nemesis—our ineptitude regarding money management. Despite running a household together for twenty-six years, Rich and I had never truly mastered our finances nor resolved our differences regarding money. A myriad of foolish decisions led us yet again into deep financial trouble.

Gratitude was soon replaced with anxiety. I feared losing the house that just a year ago had represented a new direction, a victory. I'd wake up at four in the morning with my stomach in knots worrying about how we would make it. The tension that Rich and I had experienced in the past over money grew. Something had to give.

Fear blinds us to solutions and muddles our thoughts. And in the middle of the night, it becomes the monster in the closet. We ask God for the same thing over and over again and get no answer. His seeming lack of response leaves us confounded, even angry. Why doesn't God hear our prayer? In retrospect, his silence was clearly telling me something: I was asking for the wrong thing. I prayed to God to bail us out when, in fact, he wanted Rich and me to accept responsibility and work through our money problems as a team. Like most of us, I was looking for the quick fix, for money to appear out of nowhere. God had a larger vision: to heal and strengthen our marriage through the exercise of comanaging our finances.

I began to learn that grace could not and should not be contained in a box of my own making. God means for this flow of grace to grow exponentially as we are ready to receive it. Just as the Lord's vision for our lives is far larger than we could ever imagine and his love deeper and wider than ours could ever be, so is his grace equally as powerful and transforming. God was about to unfold this lesson before us, creating a lasting foundation of trust.

I asked for the wrong thing but God revealed the right answer. I heard about Dave Ramsey, a money guru whose mission was to help people get out of debt. His book *The Total Money Makeover* laid out a plan for solving financial problems. I bought the book and announced to Rich that I wanted to try this approach. Ramsey was a no-nonsense guide with nuts-and-bolts answers. He insisted that those following his plan accept responsibility and work together to get out of debt, being keenly aware of the number of marriages that fall apart because of money issues. Having gone bankrupt, he and his wife had worked in partnership to fight their way back to solvency through hard work, common sense, and a proper focus on stewardship. Rich was skeptical but agreed to go along with the idea.

This was our beginning step toward working with God for a profound repair. For the first time I began to see why we were always in so much trouble. Ramsey's techniques offered a clear solution, one that would require both of us to be on board to tackle the hard work. Humility was required if we were to become a viable team.

After a year of following the plan, things began to improve. While emerging from debt was the desired goal, I count as the greater blessing the partnership that Rich and I formed to solve the problem. We turned from stubborn competitors to supportive soul mates. The acquisition of the kayak during this time proved to be the starting point of that lesson.

At first I had not known what I should pray for, but that didn't seem to matter. I firmly believe that God took my feeble efforts as permission to act, first by guiding us to a book that helped us make major life changes, and then by leading us to the kayak, which provided the model for harmonious teamwork.

I had looked for the "quick fix" but learned that the true solution comes through the difficult and often creative work of transformation. I discovered that often there are more profound problems lurking beneath the surface that can preclude the work from being done. Progress was slow and required patience, but each little step was bringing us closer to resolution. We began paying down our debt. I stopped waking up in the wee hours of the morning oppressed by the monster in the closet; the anxiety of financial loss was replaced with peace. Each time I was tempted by fear, I imagined myself drifting downstream in the kayak, and the fear would fade.

Grace carried us far beyond what I had asked for, taking us deep into the heart of our relationship as a married couple. For the first time in our marriage, I truly put Rich first, thinking of his needs over mine; he did the same. We wanted to be together more often and took every opportunity to do so.

The blessings came but not without tests and challenges. The path of creative transformation is part of a longer journey.

Storing Up Treasure

In reflecting on the various losses I had experienced, I know there are many things I would do differently. There is, however, one thing I would not change. Without my knowing it, over the years I had been building a storehouse of spiritual treasure that got me through my suffering without my losing faith in God. As a result, I am now a great believer in saving up for a rainy day. I can't say that such a storehouse would always guarantee the ability to hold on during a difficult season, but it is the best protection I can think of. There are times when we are literally flattened by our trials, made numb, maybe to the point of losing our faith. While I have not experienced that, I know people who have. They were in this state for a long time, unable to call on God or turn to the Church for solace. Yet even after an extended spell of such intense grief, they found their way back. I believe it was because of years of storing up spiritual treasure, the discipline that ingrained good habits. These were the concrete practices to which they could cling that led them back home. I believe my years of spiritual discipline conditioned my instinctual responses, especially during my father's illness. It's an ongoing effort to remain mindful of God at all times. I often have said to friends that should I find myself in a plane going down, I would hope to instinctively reach out to God rather than give in to fear. Stored spiritual treasures condition me to remember God at all times.

Does the word "discipline" carry a negative connotation for you? In the past I've connected it with punishment or a long list of unpleasant obligations. The delightful aspect of spiritual discipline is the opportunity for creative expression. Each of us builds our own spiritual disciplines that reflect our unique personhood. I have found mine to be not only a form of expression but a means of transforming my life, bit by bit. The end result was instinctively reaching out to God when I needed him the most.

What are my spiritual disciplines that have worked to fill my storehouse with treasure? Mine are listed here. What would yours be?

- Faithful attendance to Mass and the reception of the Eucharist

- A desire to know God personally, building on that friendship through a daily regimen of prayer throughout the day, along with reading the Bible and spiritual books

- Journaling

- Service to the Church through teaching, singing, and bringing Communion
- Building friendships with other believers and creating a network whereby we would pray for each other, especially to cover those times when we could not pray for ourselves

I would never presume to brag of great success in any of these areas; many times I fail miserably. There were many days when my disciplines felt like chores (and still do). But the *desire to persist* is constant. Once God became alive for me again, I never stopped in my pursuit. I'd fall hard from grace, then pick myself up again and continue in that pursuit. I am certain that my ingrained habits, especially that of regularly attending Mass and receiving Communion, provided the strength to persevere.

A visual comes to mind for my storehouse. I imagine it being like the Egyptian temple granaries in that scene from the movie *The Ten Commandments* when Charlton Heston as Moses breaks open those granaries so that the slaves can partake of the grain. The Egyptians stored up a lot of grain to appease their gods, but instead our God allowed the grain to pour out and feed needy people. What kinds of spiritual food do we store in our granaries so that we remain fed and feed those around us, even during the worst of trials?

Flow Lesson 3

Storing Up Spiritual Treasure through Disciplines

Materials needed: pen or pencil and paper; a table; Post-it notes (smaller size); a sturdy plastic bag; small objects to fill it up with such as stones, coins, marbles, or whatever you can find that will allow you to stick on a Post-it note

Find a table to sit at, and place your plastic bag in front of you with the Post-it notes and objects. As a way to empty your mind, look at your pile and mentally attach a thought or concern to each object. Place the object in the plastic bag as a way of putting those concerns aside so you can concentrate on being in the presence of God. Do this until you feel you have released your cares, and then sit quietly for a moment or two.

Next, empty the plastic bag onto the table. You will now assign ideas for spiritual disciplines to your objects as a way of building on your storehouse of treasure. You can start from the list in this book, but the idea is to think of things you enjoy doing that could remind you of God. Here are some ideas:

- If you love to cook for your family, pray over each part of the meal as an offering to God and your family. Cap it off by leading your family in grace at the dinner table. If this idea appeals to you, *write "meal and prayer" on your Post-it note and stick it to your object.*

- Take a hot, scented bath—a great place to pray in peace. I used to say my Rosary in the tub when the children were little—it was the only quiet room in the house! Use your imagination to link the feel of the water and the warmth to feelings you have about God. If you would like to try this idea, *write "bath" on your Post-it note and stick it to another object.*

- If you're into technology, set your Google calendar to send you an e-mail each hour during the day to remind you to offer short prayers for something in particular. It can be a mixture of petitions, praise, and thanksgivings; a quick examination of conscience; or formal prayers such as the Angelus at noon or the Divine Mercy Chaplet at three in the afternoon. Choose a bell sound on your phone to notify you, just like monks would hear at the abbey. If you like this idea, *write "Google calendar" on your Post-it note and stick it onto the next object.*

- Maybe you like to sing. Purchase a CD of favorite church hymns, contemporary Christian songs, or even popular music that would remind you of God. Take a drive and sing along, maybe even at the top of your lungs, as a prayer to God. If this idea appeals to you, *write "sing" on your Post-it note and stick it on the next object.*

- Perhaps you enjoy partaking of the rich assortment of spoken prayers offered by our Church, such as the Rosary, the Divine Mercy Chaplet, the Angelus, and the Liturgy of the Hours. It takes spiritual maturity to stick with these prayers; boredom and distractions are very real obstacles. There comes a point, however, when you able to transcend those obstacles and receive spiritual insight and consolation. If you enjoy such prayers, *write "Church prayers" on your Post-it note and stick it on the next object.*

These are just suggestions that will hopefully inspire you to come up with your own ideas when you are ready.

When you have finished labeling your objects (and don't be disturbed if you only have a few; hopefully, you will continue to add to the pile), place them all in the plastic bag. Offer your spiritual disciplines to God, and ask him to fill you with his treasures, with the promise that you will do your part to keep your disciplines. Place the bag in a prominent place as a reminder of your promise.

Overcoming the Tyranny of Emotion

One lesson learned from my season of loss is the true nature of strong emotions. I needed to acknowledge not only their presence but the control they could wield over me. I found feelings of depression, fear, and stress to be enslaving and capricious. They often blinded me to the true nature of the problems in my life and prevented me from doing the hard work necessary to work through those problems. Sometimes emotions caused me to act impulsively without thought to future consequences; other times they trapped me waste deep in mud or threatened me like that proverbial monster in the closet.

So what do we do when grief weighs so heavily upon us, causing us to burst into tears in public, or hide ourselves away in a darkened room, or lose our faith in God? What do we do when the burden of fear wakes us up in the middle of the night? What happens when we react in a way contrary to the "proper" expression of a feeling, such as in my desire to buy a house rather than to cry over my father?

While there is no one "catchall" answer to these questions, one thought comes to mind: do the opposite of what you want to do. The word *want* is the key—want is determined by emotion. As someone who is very emotional, this is hard to do! I recall one morning feeling unable to pray because I was so overwhelmed with negative emotions. I was not only sad but very angry. My inclination was to vent, to complain to God about all that was wrong. My instinct, however, told me to do the opposite—praise him. I did that by putting on my favorite spiritual music and singing along at the top of my lungs. In essence, I shouted at God! Not the laments that I wanted to shout, but scripture verses and words of praise embedded in the lyrics. That "shouting" empowered me, enabling me to plow through my negative emotions. In the midst of the shouting, God revealed to me why I was feeling so negative. It calmed the storm; my shouting fell to a whisper as peace settled in. I had not sung to God for any other purpose than to push through my negativity; the insight gained was a gift he granted.

The Growth of Grace

When we partner with God in creating our storehouse of spiritual treasure, we are, in effect, immersing ourselves in the river of grace. We are allowing grace to grow within us and fortify us. Grace opens that child's eye within, perceiving God with greater clarity. Grace conditions us to reach out to God by pure instinct when we need our Lord the most. The constant motion of grace stirs the creative pot, and this is where the adventure begins.

Grace is first planted within us through the sacraments; it grows because of the decisions we make to be open, honest, vulnerable, and trusting toward God and with each other. For Rich and me, grace extended beyond the church walls into our home, our lives, and everything we did. We learned to accept it and understand that it could come from unexpected places such as kayaks and rivers. We learned how blessings could multiply and flow between us as we remained in God's current.

Long ago, God invited the patriarch Abraham to accompany him on a grand adventure of grace that literally changed the world. As relayed in Genesis, chapters 11–25, Abraham was told by God—seemingly out of nowhere—to leave his own country; he was expected to pack up his belongings, take his wife Sarah, his nephew Lot, all of his servants and cattle, and travel to a new land that God would then give to him. Abraham set off even though he was not afforded any foreknowledge of the land to which he was headed; he was only given the guidance needed to make the journey.

Through a vision, the Lord promised Abraham numerous descendants even though Abraham and his wife were childless and elderly at the time. Abraham asked God for a son, and God responded by blessing Sarah's barren womb. That son, Isaac, would be the beginning of a line of descendants, which would form many nations, but not before Abraham was put to the test. When asked to sacrifice his only son, Abraham did not openly question. While scripture does not tell us what went on inside of him, I imagine that as a father Abraham felt alarmed and perplexed. I picture Abraham fighting through any doubt, dread, or sorrow in order to comply—only to be stopped by the intervention of an angel. Even though Abraham did not understand God's request, even though that request likely caused anguish, Abraham chose to trust God. That trust was rewarded by the fulfillment of God's promises to him.

Abraham's story is a call to our own stories, and it reveals many aspects of grace. First, it began with the invitation from God to be in relationship with him. The flow of grace grew stronger as Abraham opened up his heart to God and learned to trust him. For all of us, learning to trust in God allows us to be carried in his grace. Abraham did not fret about the future but was content to be led by God, step by step, day by day. Although Abraham asked for only one thing, a son, God multiplied that blessing with descendants too numerous to count.

The lessons I've learned from Abraham are lessons in trusting God, leading to a wider vision for my life. There's also something to keep in mind. Scripture is clear that God tested Abraham—and with an impossible request—but God intervened when he knew Abraham trusted him.

The losses I have experienced, first with my father's death, and then with our mounting debt, produced questions which led to a fundamental shift in my faith. Perhaps in your losses, you too have thought of these questions:

- Am I aware of the role of grace in my life?

- Am I cognizant of its flow?

- Where has grace taken me?

- How have I gotten there? Would I have gone had I known in advance what I would experience?

- Am I grateful to be where I am today as result of grace?

If I had known what lay ahead of me, I might not have had the courage to go along with the flow; I might have lost faith. I am grateful to God for revealing to me what I needed to know one day at a time so that I could persevere.

Living by faith involves not knowing what lies ahead. The writer E. L. Doctorow reflects on the process of moving into the unknown with respect to writing a novel. I consider what he says about writing a novel is also true of living by faith: "Writing a novel can be like driving at night—you can only see as far as your headlights will allow."[3] You can't see far ahead, but you can reach your destination like that. Being limited in our long–range vision allows us to see all that God wants to reveal right in front of us. Projecting into the future robs us of those small details and creates needless anxiety.

I've learned to slow down and appreciate the seemingly small stuff, for often, it's not small at all. How easy it was for me to see the Communion host as just a humble wafer in appearance, when in actuality it is the Body and Blood of Jesus Christ. Now instead of taking it in a rush or without thought, I look at it for a moment before consuming and think about the act of eating it as I contemplate the astonishing intimacy that Jesus affords me through its consumption. My imagination comes alive in the contemplation. Living in the present moment rather than worrying about where I will be an hour from now affords me the opportunity to see what God means to reveal to me.

These things were a prelude to events that were about to unfold in our lives. Over the next several years, Rich and I would each experience a transformation that would send us on a new course both as individuals and as a couple. It would mean the shedding of an old and complacent lifestyle and require all the love, courage, and trust that we could muster. It would prove to be a new set of amazing adventures.

Questions for Reflection

1. What words would you use to describe grace? Where do you find grace in your life?

2. Describe a specific incident where you experienced a personal encounter with God. What did it feel like? Did it change you? Do you consider that to be a grace? Do you think you can experience such an encounter again? Why or why not?

3. Do you equate God with the everyday? Can you describe something concrete in your life that connects you with truths about God?

4. How has fear kept you bound? Can you name your fears? How can naming your fears help you to overcome them?

5. How has grace affected your closest relationships? Describe one such relationship and how grace has caused it to grow and change.

6. What words and feelings immediately come to mind when you hear the word "obedience"? Why do you feel that way? Do you associate it with "no" or with "yes"?

Visit beasone.org, click on the "Resources" tab and then "Flow Lessons" for additional activities to facilitate a deeper exploration of the concepts of this chapter. Videos, music, and examples are supplied to help you with these exercises.

Chapter 2—Allowing Grace to Grow

How Dealing with My Mother's Death Helped Me Cope with Fear

When my husband and I first took up kayaking, we enjoyed many leisurely trips together in our tandem kayak. Eventually Rich took up fishing (a sport I'm not drawn to) and got a kayak that seats one. Since we both loved the water, it made sense for me also to have a smaller kayak. It afforded me the opportunity to go out as often as I wished, but I missed that connection we built and experienced when going out in the tandem.

That simple metaphor comes to mind when I recall my mother's illness and death; ultimately, she chose to go it alone, with a self-imposed isolation from family and friends that created an emotional suffering far surpassing her physical pain. While the single kayak wasn't a severe split like that, it was a loss, giving me a concrete image for better understanding my mother's choices.

Her journey taught me valuable lessons about the necessity of being connected to others that I will never forget. It gave me a new empathy with those who are suffering and a sense of urgency to forge my own connections. Ultimately, it showed me that love must and can overcome the power of fear.

Many of us have experienced the loss of one or both of our parents. Some of us were close to our mother or father, while others of us were estranged. For those whose parents are still living, the thought of losing them can be hard to imagine, especially if we know our parents as friends, sharing together in our dreams, successes, hurts, and losses.

My relationship with my mother was like that: she was my best friend and confidant. She passed down to me her love of learning and appreciation for nature, especially birds. She taught me the value of courtesy and the importance of treating others the way I would wish to be treated. She had a never-ending enthusiasm for life that was infectious. Now I work to emulate her thoughtfulness and kindness. Her unwavering commitment to her children inspired me to have the same.

My mother's downturn began with the death of my father in December 2003. After my father breathed his last, she remained with him, cradling his head in her arms for some time. The look of disbelief on her face was heartbreaking. In their fifty-four years of marriage, they raised three children together, remaining intimately involved in all aspects of our lives. They shared travels and a deep love of nature. Together they endured the heartache of my brother's prolonged illness but also reveled in their grandchildren. Despite opposite temperaments and hot disagreements, my parents were inseparable companions with their shared interests, values, and beliefs. The blunt trauma of losing the love of her life broke my mother's spirit, signaling the beginning of her slow decline.

Because of advancing dementia, she began to lose the ability to control her inner thoughts and feelings, and the pain in her life and "evils" in her soul poured out in a torrent. Since she was a proud woman, exposing herself in that way must have been mortifying and excruciating. Feeling unworthy of love, she began to cut herself off from her friends and church community; she expressed her self-hatred by lashing out at those around her, including her family.

The darkness that became my mother's constant companion became ours as well, affecting our behavior and judgment regarding the proper care of her needs. It took an intervention from an attentive VA nurse to open our eyes to the true extent of our mother's physical needs, talking us through the necessary steps to secure my mother in a better situation. Simple measures were taken to assure that she would be fed, clothed, and bathed. But how could we address her emotional, social, and spiritual needs? A kiss on the forehead, a hug, saying "I love you"—we became afraid to offer even these things.

Part of grieving is looking back at not only the people we have lost but how we feel we may have failed them at some level. Although we were a loving and close family, the very notions of physical affection or just saying "I love you" were unthinkable. I regretted not having prayed to God for the strength to overcome those inhibitions; surely I had already begun to understand that the river of grace would enable me to do the seemingly impossible. At the time however, I could not see it; it was all any of us could do just to hang on.

Moments of crises tend to reveal our greatest strengths and most troubling weaknesses. Some of us will choose to run away, while others will run straight into the fire. My mother's emotional turmoil and dementia terrified me, and I found myself blinded by fear. Just as with my own family's money crisis, once again I became fixated in my petitions to God. I prayed for her soul in desperate pleas, but I couldn't find my way to ask God for the grace to see and meet her most immediate needs. The river of grace seemed to slow to a trickle, and I was the culprit, cutting off the flow because I refused to face my fear.

I became overwhelmed with a sense of inadequacy as I watched my sister and brother provide for my mother's physical and material needs in such a capable way. Fear blinded me to my true role, one that was equally as important: providing the simple comfort of my presence. My sister understood that inherently and gently reminded me that I needed to spend more time with my mother, to listen and to console her.

Flow Lesson 4

Releasing Our Regrets

Materials needed: pen or pencil and paper; a large sink or bathtub; a small, empty Tupperware container; various small objects that will not be harmed should they get wet

Note: Making use of the Sacrament of Reconciliation is the best place to start when dealing with regrets. The kind counsel of the priest coupled with the reception of sanctifying grace provides true spiritual healing. The value of this exercise is for any leftover regrets you were unable to release after reception of the sacrament.

This may be a difficult exercise, so you will want to take some extra time to be in the presence of God. Use previous practices such as breathing slowly, imagining birds flying away from a tree, or placing objects in a bag to clear your mind of cares and anxieties.

There are times in our lives when we feel we have fallen short in our actions, failing to do our best for someone we love or even doing something that caused harm to that person. This can cause a tremendous burden of guilt and regret. Even if others disagree with our assessment of our actions, our own perception is what is real to us. We may have even already confessed our shortfall but still feel burdened with regret. With all this in mind, take a moment to recall any regrets in your life with regard to failing someone you loved (just as I regretted not being more present to my mother's immediate needs). Write them down.

Regrets are burdens that need to be unloaded and released; this exercise will provide a concrete means to do so. Taking your list, go to the sink or bathtub and fill it with water (consider using the bathtub since it will make the exercise more effective). Take a small Tupperware container and place it in the water. Have your objects in a pile next to your paper. Pick up an object and assign it something from your list, speaking that something out loud. For example: "I would not kiss my mother." Place the object in the container. Do this for every item on your list. After doing so, place your list in the container as well.

Pull the Tupperware toward the edge of the sink or bathtub (in essence, anchoring it). Closing your eyes, imagine yourself sitting on a dock next to Jesus, leaning in to him. You and he are swinging your feet over a large barge filled to the brim with heavy rubble. Imagine looking into Jesus' eyes and saying the following prayer: "Lord Jesus Christ, Son of God, have mercy on me, a sinner." Say this prayer out loud several times. As you say the prayer, imagine the Lord pointing to your feet and instructing you to place them on the rim of the barge; he is doing the same. Imagine yourself pushing the barge away with the Lord and watching it float downstream and out of sight.

Open your eyes and release your container, pushing it slowly away—in effect releasing all of those objects labeled with your regrets. As you watch it float away, say, "Thank you, Jesus, for releasing my burden," for each object in that container (even if that thank-you does not yet feel genuine).

Take a moment to be still with God, and reflect upon what has just occurred. If you feel so inclined, write down your impressions. Thank God for forgiving you and for taking from you the burden of your regrets.

Becoming a Dealer

Emotional, social, and spiritual aspects of illness are harder to grasp and, as a result, are often summarily dismissed. Dr. Daniel Hinshaw, in his book *Suffering and the Nature of Healing*, writes, "By their nature, emotional, social, or spiritual experiences of the patient or caregiver are subjective and qualitative. . . . They are not 'scientific' and therefore are basically suspect. Inevitably, the emphasis on the objective/scientific approach has shifted the focus of medical effort to disease as a target of treatment and away from the person. As a consequence, a mind-body disconnect has developed in Western modern medicine."[1]

The Great Physician did not practice with such a mindset; instead, he dealt with the *whole* person. In taking the time to discern each person's true needs, from social and emotional to spiritual and physical, Jesus employed considerable creativity as a healer. In this way the restoration that the Great Physician brought to his patients transformed their lives. We too can bring healing, being Jesus to others. The gospels provide us with many wonderful examples:

- *Rather than impose himself, Jesus respected the person's wishes,* as with the Roman centurion in Matthew 8 who did not feel worthy enough for Jesus to enter his home. In this case, less was definitely more. Jesus' kindness in healing the centurion's servant from afar likely planted a seed of love along with gratitude. In what ways can we respect a person's wishes for distance and still be a healing presence for them? One time when I needed to spend a whole day with my mother, I decided to bring my laptop and do some work while I sat with her. The fact that I was busy with something granted my mother the "distance" she wanted until she was ready to talk. That time of just being in the same room together caused her eventually to let down her guard. We spent the rest of the afternoon reminiscing and sharing a meal together. It was a rare moment in her seven years of suffering and a gift that she left for me to cherish.

• *When permitted, Jesus touched the sick person, sometimes making primitive balms to help,* as in the case of applying mud to the blind man's eyes using Jesus' own spittle in John 9. Jesus was certainly creative in his method and bold in his application of the cure since there was no guarantee the man would accept it. It required an intimate form of touch which literally transformed the man from blind to seeing. Just how important is that level of intimacy? I recall a phone conversation I had with my mother near the end of her life. She had trouble conversing, so on the spur of the moment I said, "I love you, Mommy." There was a pregnant pause before she replied, "I love you, too." We had never spoken that way to each other before. My taking the chance to say I loved her caused her to do the same.

• *Jesus drew the sick person out of the shadows of shame and ostracism,* as with his calling out the hemorrhaging woman who had touched his cloak in secret and who was healed in Luke 8. That woman's life was transformed from one of shame, loneliness, and secrecy to one of openness and acceptance back into the community. Is it possible to console someone in their shame and misery, to enfold them back into the community, simply by being present to them? When I visited my mother during the dinner hour at the nursing home, I noticed she regularly dined with another resident, a woman with Alzheimer's, and her daughter, Sandy. Because she was present to my mother during those meals, Sandy was able to see through my mother's fear, anger, and despair to the intelligent, feisty, witty, and caring woman hidden underneath. After my mother passed away, I called Sandy and told her what it meant to me that she befriended my mother, choosing to see her as a whole person rather than as a ravaged, bitter woman. The continued presence of Sandy and her mother at the table each night offered my mother companionship and a chance to be part of a community.

• *Jesus tended to the person's spiritual sickness as well as his physical needs* by first forgiving the sins of the paralytic and then healing him physically in Mark 2. This man's companions employed creative means, carefully lowering their friend on a mat through the ceiling so that he could see Jesus. Their act of love was rewarded with the man's healing both spiritually and physically. They played a part in their friend's life being transformed. But what if someone, like my mother, is hostile to any talk of religion? What creative means can be used to demonstrate the love of God? Faithfulness in doing her grocery shopping was one way I could be Jesus to my mother and show her my love. By investing the time and patience needed to help her make the list and then getting exactly what she wanted, I was able to fulfill an important need. Every now and then I would throw in a surprise treat that she could enjoy. We don't always see how such actions play out so, we must persevere and trust that God will use our actions.

The gospels show our Lord valuing all aspects of each sick person he encountered, resulting in a total healing of that person. He sought to create a relationship and overcame any fear through his love for that person. The foundation of the Great Physician's creative and transformative healings was a loving relationship.

Flow Lesson 5

Becoming Instruments of Healing

Materials needed: pen or pencil and paper; bible

Take a moment to become still before God. Ask the Holy Spirit to grant insight and wisdom for this exercise.

In this exercise you will first examine one of the healing stories from the Bible and explore how Jesus restored the sick person and how others played a role in that restoration. After prayerful consideration of the story, you will then look to your own situation as either a caregiver or as someone who is in need of healing and draw parallels between your story and the one you read in the Bible.

Take two pieces of paper; title one page "Gospel Story" and the other "My Story."

Next, choose one of the healing stories just discussed and read the entire story from the Bible:

- The Roman centurion: Matthew 8:5–13

- The blind man: John 9:1–12

- The hemorrhaging woman: Luke 8:40–48
- The paralytic: Mark 2:1–12

After reading the story, consider these questions and write down your answers on the page labeled "Bible Story":

1. Other than Jesus, who was the main character of the story? What made him or her central to the story?

2. Who are the minor characters? List them and describe their roles. What were their relationships to the main character?

3. If the main character was not the person in need of healing, what role did that character play in helping that person to receive healing?

4. What did Jesus do to build a relationship with the sick person? How did that person respond?

5. What means did Jesus use to heal that person? How do you think the healing transformed the life of that person? If you were that person, how do you think your life would have been transformed?

6. Beyond the physical healing, what evidence of emotional, social, or spiritual healing do you see in the story?

7. Who represents the community in the story? Remember that a community only needs to consist of one or two other persons. What role does the community play? Are they helpful? Do they ask questions? Are they a hindrance? Do they just witness the healing? How does Jesus engage the community?

Go back over the questions and your notes. Do you see any parallels to your own life story? If you do, write them down. If you do not as of yet, do not be concerned because the answers may come at a later point.

Before proceeding to the next part of this exercise, take a few moments to be still with God and let the story and your reflections sink in. Imagine the story taking place in your mind as you assume various roles: the sick person receiving the healing, Jesus offering the healing, the other players either helping the sick person to receive the healing or witnessing the miracle. As you imagine these scenes, ask God to reveal to you what he wants you to know.

Now consider these questions tailored more to your story:

1. Who is the person in your story that is in need of healing? Is it you? What kind of healing is needed?

2. Who are the minor characters in your story? List them. What roles do they play? Are they helpful, a hindrance, or merely bystanders?

3. If the main character in your story is you, and you are not in need of healing, what role do you play in helping your loved one to receive healing? Looking back over the examples I gave, what creative ways do you employ to bring healing into the life of your loved one? For example, have you prayed for him or her? Have you kept him or her company or kept up the house for him or her? Do you manage his or her finances and arrange for caregivers? Do you bring Communion to that person?

4. Describe your relationship with the person you are caring for, or, if you are the one receiving care, describe your relationship with your caregiver. Is the relationship loving and helpful, hurtful and combative, or somewhere in between? Does the relationship resemble how Jesus related to the sick, and if not, what can you do to bring healing to the relationship?

5. If you are in need of healing, what have your prayer requests been? Do you feel you have received any answers, and if so,

what are they? If you are caring for someone else, have you
seen answers to your prayers for him or her, and if so, what
are those answers?

6. Have you witnessed any physical healing for either yourself
   or your loved one? Describe what happened. For example, is
   the pain less severe? Has a cancer gone into remission? Is a
   new medication working more effectively? Has there been any
   emotional, social, or spiritual healing in your story? Has the
   person made peace with his or her situation? Is that person
   turning to God for help? Has that person stayed in touch with
   family and friends?

      As this exercise comes to an end, take a few moments to
be quiet again with the Lord. Reflect again on the gospel story
and also on your story: Do you see any parallels? If you do, write
them down. Ask the Lord to help you be more like Jesus to the
person you are caring for or to your caregiver. Take your notes
and place them where you will see them, and offer them daily
to the Lord, asking to be made more like him.

Letting Love Overcome Fear

It is one thing to be told to imitate our Lord and another to do
it. Although I was keenly aware of my mother's emotional, social,
and spiritual needs, I was unable for a long time to act upon that
knowledge. I needed God's grace to release the power of love to
overcome fear. I see now that grace could have enabled me to
forget myself and reach out, so long as I believed in its power.

      Were I to relive that time in my life, I would actively seek
out grace through the sacraments, especially the Sacrament of
Reconciliation. The concrete and formal nature of the sacraments

is a wonderful gift of our Church, particularly during those times of crises. There we encounter Jesus as friend and Great Physician, present to us through the auspices of the priest, the ritual, the words of absolution, and the community. We are given healing and strength through grace, and we can pass that along to those we care for.

I cannot relive that time, and I have had to let go of my regrets. But I can be better prepared for those others for whom I will be asked to care because of what God has revealed to me through these experiences. I may not have been everything I wished for during my mother's illness, but the graces received and lessons learned can be used for others.

Jesus, as the Great Physician, was not afraid. Many of the sick whom Jesus healed were possessed by demons, or lepers—those whose diseases generated the most fear. In the story of the man cleansed of evil spirits in Mark's gospel (5:1–20), we see a wild man who lived among the tombs, screaming and causing physical harm to himself. Townspeople were terrified of him because he could not be contained. The demons that possessed him recognized the divinity of Jesus and begged Jesus to send them into a herd of swine. Subsequently, they rushed off the side of the mountain and into the lake to drown.

In his book *Jesus: A Pilgrimage*, Fr. James Martin, S.J., reflects on the demoniac: "It is easy to hear in this story echoes of people we know who seem intent on harming themselves, and indeed anyone who engages in self-destructive behavior through addictions, compulsions or habits. Probably the man desperately wanted to be free of these demons, but had no idea how to free himself. His cries . . . are those not just of a frightening man, but of a frightened man."[2]

When we hurt or see others hurting, we often self-protect, pushing loved ones away, even as we harm ourselves and

others with our words and actions. But still taking one small
step toward communion—community—is a valued action we
take toward others. The act of love, no matter how small—right
down to whether or not we smile and make eye contact with
them—is important. St. Thérèse of Lisieux was known for the
little things she did to bring light and cheer to her fellow sisters.
She recounts in the story of her care of an elderly nun: "I soon
noticed that she found it very difficult to cut her bread, so I did
not leave her till I had performed this last service. She was much
touched by this attention on my part, for she had not expressed
any wish on the subject; it was by this unsought-for kindness
that I gained her entire confidence, and chiefly because—as I
learned later—at the end of my humble task I bestowed upon
her my sweetest smile."[3]

Cutting a person's bread. Offering smiles no matter what
the mood of the person. Grocery shopping, getting exactly
what the person wants. Remembering happier times by going
through old photo albums or just reminiscing. Telling funny
stories. Watching television together. Reading the newspaper or
a book out loud. Helping to write a letter or address Christmas
cards to send. Bringing Communion, reading a favorite psalm
out loud, praying the Rosary or the Divine Mercy Chaplet if a
person is religiously minded. Just sitting and listening. I see now
that there are so many little ways to care for a person's emotional,
social, and spiritual needs. As shown by St. Thérèse's example,
small gestures mean the world when they are given out of love.

My sister understood the power of small gestures in making connections. She wrote, "Two days before [Mommy] died I
tried to say 'I love you' to my mother but all that came out was
'It's so hard . . . ,' stopping because I was choked up with tears.
Parents and children communicate so effectively non-verbally.

Just a look, a gesture can say so much. She turned to me in a morphine haze and in her eyes was unconditional love."

Grace is fueled by love. Love can overcome fear if we face that fear head on. Spending more time with my mother reminded me of my love for her, giving me the strength to forget my fear. In time I began to find little ways to help. I was able to interpret her random thoughts and help her express herself as dementia ate away at her ability to remember words. As I mentioned, I took over the grocery shopping. I told her I loved her. I visited her regularly even as fear and dread accompanied me. I prayed for her constantly. I handled the funeral arrangements and sang her favorite song at the service.

Because of her rejection of religion, we could only pray for her. Still, when she ended up in the emergency room with congestive heart failure and the doctor asked if we wanted to contact a priest, I called on Fr. Giggi, who had been so kind to our family during our father's illness and who was the one clergy member my mother trusted.

Days later my mother was sent back to the nursing home into hospice care. Despite the morphine she was restless. Her eyes were hollow and terror stricken. We felt helpless. During my last visit with her, I whispered into her ear, "Leave the door open. Someone is waiting for you on the other side. Someone who loves you very much! Leave open the possibility!" It seemed impossible that she could have understood what I was trying to tell her. Still, I placed my trust in God's grace.

The day of her funeral dawned bright with warm sunshine, blooming flowers, and budding trees full of singing birds. Spring had always been her favorite season, and it had come early that year, a poetic gesture since my mother had devoted much of her life to the outdoors. The chapel was filled with family and friends, and a stream of tributes began. As I listened to people sharing their stories, I knew my mother had loved well even if she didn't believe it herself. After the service I walked up to the casket draped in luxuriant purple and white flowers, kissed it, pointed to it, and said, "See, I told you you were loved!" In my heart I sensed the words "Love begets love." I interpreted this as the first of several signs to come assuring me that my deepest desire was realized. Had the message to be open to the prospect of God gotten through? God's ways defy understanding; we cannot ever hope to know him with certainty. Instead he gives us faith such that our hearts can discern his mercy and grace. The gift is there right in front of us, waiting to be received. I felt certain God had granted mercy to my mother in answer to my prayers, and I claimed that gift, recalling the acts of mercy Jesus practiced during his time on earth.

As I think of and pray for my mother now, I ask God often that I may remain mindful of him and those around me, whatever the circumstance. Whenever I have the slightest pain or ailment, I seek out the company of God, even if I do not feel him near me. It's something I work at, and I trust it will lay the foundation for a habit that will serve me when the cross truly gets heavy.

Practicing the Presence of God

Remaining aware of God takes practice; it is the fruit of spiritual disciplines, much like the ones suggested in the aforementioned Flow Lesson in chapter 1. Using my iPhone to remind me hourly to pray has probably been the most helpful in creating this mindfulness. Since I always have my phone with me, I never miss the e-mail reminders. It can be hard to stop what I am doing to pray, even for just a few seconds, but the result is a constant reminder of God's presence. It's not unlike the Divine Office that priests and religious pray at certain times of the day—the idea is to be in a constant state of prayer. The habit of praying acts as a catalyst that snaps my mind to attention, placing me instantaneously in God's presence. This discipline has taught me that mindfulness of God is, in fact, praying without ceasing.

Creating a sacred space is also an effective catalyst. Any place can be a sacred space requiring just a few simple accoutrements. I made my car into such a space by placing three small icons of Jesus, Mary, and the Holy Trinity on my dashboard. I now consider my long commute to be a gift of time with God when I can pray the Rosary, listen to music or a podcast, talk to God, or just be quiet and listen. A rosary ring makes it easier (and safer) to pray the Rosary and drive at the same time.

Building such habits taps into your creativity as you come up with fresh ideas that will turn you toward God. The more you explore various disciplines, the more you exercise that creative muscle. The formation of these disciplines has transformed my prayer life in an amazing way. What began as small repetitive acts done out of obligation have become rituals that I cherish. As a result, I am more aware of the present moment and thus can perceive God with greater clarity.

A prayerful state can be especially hard to attain when you are in pain and it seems consolation will never come. The temptation to turn inward and disconnect can be overwhelming. When we feel that way, concrete reminders can suggest that God is near. Particularly in the middle of the night, I find these things helpful:

- clutching a rosary in my hand

- gazing at a picture of Mary—if you wake at night in a panic, her image can offer surprising comfort

- repeating the Jesus Prayer ("Lord Jesus Christ, son of God, have mercy on me, a sinner")—this creates a rhythm that can bring peace

- listening to spiritual music

One lesson I will never forget during my parents' illnesses was the importance of asking family and friends for their prayers. There were times when I just could not put the words together; therefore, knowing prayers were being said for us acted as an assurance that God was near.

When we are in pain, we can feel that God has abandoned us. I am reminded of Mother Teresa's years of darkness during the time she served the poor in Calcutta. When she could no longer depend on an emotional connection, she relied upon her steadfast belief that Jesus was with her, even though she felt no intimacy with him. Considering the intensity of her mystical experiences with him (experiences which led her to her mission), this prolonged lack of emotional connection must have been devastating. Reaching out to her spiritual director and using writing as a means of expressing herself (as revealed in the book *Come Be My Light*) helped Mother Teresa to navigate through her darkness.[4] Her various spiritual disciplines, especially that of spending an hour a day in adoration before the Eucharist, fortified her belief. Remembering her countenance—a face beaming in love—demonstrated to me that I *can know* God is near even if I can't feel it.

Mother Teresa's pain was not meant to be hers alone. Her darkness has taught and inspired others in their faith journeys. This is how I feel about my mother's suffering—it was not in vain. By witnessing her suffering, I became acutely aware of the need to live in the present moment. I realized that *now* is the time to learn to resist the impulses of pride, stoicism, a clinging to independence, an insistence on having things my own way, and a resistance to change. *Now* is the time to learn how to accept help while at the same time remaining ever mindful of those around me and of God inside of me.

Illness and loss can draw some of us into solitude. Since I already have a strong preference for solitude, I knew that, if left unchecked, it could lead to isolation and despair. Suffering, whether it is from illness or grief, can draw us into a delusional bubble, a place where we create our own reality. Viable connections to others keep us in the real world; such connections are truly life-giving. In understanding this about myself, I vowed to change my actions. I took the first step only two weeks after my mother passed away.

Our parish was looking for Eucharistic ministers to take Communion to the homebound, so I offered to help. Julie, the parish nurse, introduced me to Jackie, who suffers from Ménière's, a chronic disease of the inner ear. Ménière's produces a sensation of extreme vertigo, which can be mitigated only by the person lying still with her eyes closed. Jackie suffers from varying degrees of nausea and dizziness plus the periodic discouragement that accompanies this kind of disease. Once active in the parish and community, she had become homebound because of the disease.

Julie sensed that Jackie and I would hit it off, and she was right: we became fast friends. Normally bringing Communion to someone requires a short visit, but typically our time together would last two hours or more. We relished every moment together. Sharing many interests in common, we found ourselves on the same wavelength when it came to the spiritual life. We loved talking about our relationship with God, how we prayed, what our faith meant to us, and how it helped us. Coincidentally, we share an interest in bird watching, something I had shared with my mother. The friendship between us felt warm and familiar. I soon adopted her as my spiritual mother.

As before with buying the house, dealing with my grief over my mother manifested itself in action. I'm not even sure why I was attracted to the advertisement in our parish bulletin about taking Communion to the homebound; I just knew the attraction was strong. St. Thérèse of Lisieux knew the power of attraction, particularly of one's desire to receive Christ in the Eucharist. She urged an individual to "receive Communion often, very often . . . Jesus has not put this attraction in your heart for nothing."[5] Here I was being given an opportunity to bring Christ to someone in need. I had no idea what that would entail or the shower of blessings that would come as a result. I just knew I had to act.

Each time I approached the tabernacle, opened it, and took out a host to bring to my friend, I marveled at the privilege of doing as the priest would do—genuflecting before the tabernacle, unlocking the gold door, and taking out the Body and Blood of Christ. I could hold the host in my hand, gaze at it with reverence, and ask for his mercy. I could meditate on the host, contemplating the mystery of holding him in my hand while knowing that, simultaneously, he was present all around me and within me. I was able to carry Jesus with me to someone who was ill and later say, "The Body of Christ," while placing the host in her hand. By still being able to receive the Eucharist, a viable connection was maintained for Jackie with our parish community. It also was a first step toward my making new and life-changing connections with others.

If I can be a Eucharistic minister, anyone can. There is nothing about me that makes me worthy of this task. I can't even sit through an hour of adoration without falling asleep. We are chosen to act on something not because we are the best at it or the most qualified; often we are chosen for the opposite reason. I believe God placed a desire in me to bring Communion to

Jackie because he wanted to help me grow despite my weakness. In asking God to help me connect with the world around me, he placed a suggestion in my mind: start with one person.

It is the little acts that have the lasting ramifications. They are the acts unseen and unsung by the world and cherished by God. There is no greater privilege than to have shown love to someone else, no matter how ordinary that show of love may be. John F. Russell, O.Carm., writes this about the little way of St. Thérèse:

> St. Thérèse translated "the little way" in terms of a commitment to the tasks and to the people we meet in our everyday lives. She took her assignments in the convent of Lisieux as ways of manifesting her love for God and for others. She worked as a sacristan by taking care of the altar and the chapel; she served in the refectory and in the laundry room; she wrote plays for the entertainment of the community. Above all, she tried to show a love for all the nuns in the community. She played no favorites; she gave of herself even to the difficult members. Her life sounds so routine and ordinary, but it was steeped in a loving commitment that knew no breakdown. It is called a little way precisely by being simple, direct, yet calling for amazing fortitude and commitment.[6]

It has occurred to me upon reflection that I had performed such little acts for my mother out of love. Perhaps I did not fail her as much as I had thought.

I often wonder about the gift God gave me through Jackie, who filled a void left behind by my mother's death. Every time I think of the many blessings I have received from knowing Jackie, I think of Jesus saying, "A good measure, pressed down, shaken together, running over, will be put into your lap; for the measure you give will be the measure you get back." He continues, "Give, and it will be given to you" (Lk 6:38). The blessings multiply until we can no longer contain them, and then we are compelled to give them away; this is the essence of the river of grace.

I had agreed to bring Communion to Jackie as a way of forging new connections. I never realized just how much this woman would teach me, especially about being mindful of God at all times, and living well in the present moment. Through her daily struggles with Ménière's, I witnessed the many small yet creative ways she seeks to remain connected to others. While each act involves great physical and emotional effort, Jackie gives life to herself and others, whether it is through her cooking, going out to lunch with friends, visiting a loved one in the nursing home, or remaining involved with our parish's bereavement group by taking charge of the mailings. Although suffering dominates and controls her life, Jackie does not allow it to define who she is. She is still Jackie: the mother, grandmother, and friend.

As my life has been transformed over the last five years, Jackie has been a mentor and friend. And although she does not consider herself to be creative, she has inherently understood my artistic side. A good portion of our conversations consists of sharing the many creative ways we draw close to God. She has taught me about spiritual communion, that act of envisioning myself receiving the host even as she physically receives it. I've learned about the viability of mental prayer, of simply sitting still and "thinking about Jesus." It reminds me of a quotation from St. Thérèse: "I went behind my bed in an empty space . . . . and . . . 'I *thought!*' . . . I think about God, about life, about ETERNITY. . . . I *think!*"[7] Sometimes I bring my guitar and play songs for Jackie, but one of the more important things I have learned how to do is just to sit and listen as she shares the pain of her illness, realizing that sometimes she just needs a safe haven where she can unburden.

So many of the common and ordinary things we take for granted end up giving life to others. It's really just a matter of taking the time. Just as I spent afternoons with my mother, giving her the time to relax and talk with me, now I spend afternoons with someone I consider my "spiritual mother." From smiles and laughter to learning and insight, from tears and pain to brief moments of prayerful silence—love is teaching me to slow down and spend the time, to drink in every single moment of grace. In my loss, God graced me with a profound gift of friendship and mentorship. The poetry of this relationship is that it revolves around the Eucharist, given and received.

A Parting Gift

Part of being in the flow of the river of grace comes from a mindfulness and connectedness, being willing to make those connections—such as saying yes to kayaking with Rich, yes to bringing the Eucharist to Jackie, yes to spending time with my mother despite my fear. Empathy requires more from us than feeling the pain of others; we must respond to that pain, and believe that love trumps fear. With my mother I was just beginning to learn how to do this, and now I am committed to remaining empathetic with everyone I meet, allowing grace to grow within me. I consider that to be one of my mother's parting gifts.

Questions for Reflection

1. Have you lost someone close to you within the last few years? Were you a caregiver to your loved one, and if so, did you

struggle with that role? What were those struggles? Do you have any regrets, and if so, what steps can you take to provide yourself a way to deal with them? Reflect on some of the little things you did for your ailing parent or loved one to minister to his or her needs. How did that parent or one in your care respond to your actions? How did that make you feel?

2. When you are ill, do you prefer the company of others or would you rather be alone? Do you allow people to take care of you? If not, how can you open the door to that care? Are you able to pray when you are in pain? Do you ask others to pray for you? If not, can you think of someone to whom you can go for prayers? What conscious steps can you take to assure that you will remain connected with God and with others?

3. How do you cope with a loved one who has lost his or her faith? How does it make you feel? What steps can you take to minister to your loved one? What can you do to replenish your own strength during this difficult time?

4. Are there lessons that you learned from caring for your loved one? Reflect upon one lesson and the effect it had on your life. What did you learn and how did it change you?

5. Can you recall a time when God surprised you with an unexpected blessing? Did it change your life in any way? What was that blessing and how did it make you feel?

Visit beasone.org, click on the "Resources" tab and then "Flow Lessons" for additional activities to facilitate a deeper exploration of the concepts of this chapter. Videos, music, and examples are supplied to help you with these exercises.

Chapter 3—Flowing with the Current

How the Loss of My Singing Voice Taught Me to Let Go

Most times when I take the kayak out, the trips are serene and uneventful. While I favor paddling in quiet streams and lakes, I will sometimes run up against opposition: a stiff wind, a sudden change in current, or motor boats racing past me and churning up waves that slam the kayak on both sides. Each time the same lesson is reinforced: there is no point in fighting the wind, the current, or the waves. The trip is a lot better when I yield to the elements.

Loss is a significant challenge, and the natural inclination is to fight it. We deny our loss and struggle against a myriad of emotions. It's one thing to lose a loved one; it's another to lose a significant part of yourself. The grief is deep in any case. Losing a loved one, however, is a more black-and-white experience: there is no argument about whether or not that person is gone. When you lose a part of yourself, however, it can get into murky areas, especially if the loss is not immediately visible to those around you. Family and friends may not appreciate or understand the depth of your loss, adding a whole other dimension to your grief.

Ecclesiastes 3 sets the stage for these kinds of challenges: the flow back and forth between the gains and losses in our lives. The writer tells us they are appointed by God: "For everything there is a season, and a time for every matter under heaven" (Eccl 3:1). There is a cyclical, temporary nature to life, the full knowledge of which belongs to the Creator alone. As we cannot ever hope to comprehend the magnitude of God, so we cannot hope to fully understand the life he has given to us. In Matthew 24:35, Jesus put forth the only permanence we can count upon: "Heaven and earth will pass away, but my words will not pass away." We may not be able to control our lives, but we can determine how we will react. Will we fight or will we yield?

Just a few months after the death of my mother, I was faced with another loss of a physical nature. The challenge of Ecclesiastes 3 was playing out: ". . . a time to kill, and a time to heal; a time to break down, and a time to build up . . . a time to embrace, and a time to refrain from embracing" (Eccl 3:3, 5b). It was a time of rejection and pushing back, anger and frustration—and then epiphany, reconciliation, and healing. This was my four-year journey that began with the discovery of a weakness in my otherwise rock-solid singing voice.

I had poured everything I had into music during my adult life. The result was a fulfilling professional career spanning fourteen years, which included singing, songwriting, and recording CDs of faith-based music. I was fortunate to have appeared on major Catholic media outlets EWTN and CatholicTV. I also had the privilege of performing at World Youth Day in Toronto in 2002, a gathering of thousands of teenagers from around the world.

It always happened in front of a crowd; sometimes my voice was strong and clear, and other times it was wobbly and erratic. My throat would tighten and become sore after only a few moments of singing. A visit to an ear, nose, and throat specialist revealed that several health issues combined to affect my voice, including a blood vessel like a bruise on my vocal chords and a condition called GERD (acid reflux disease).

The cornerstone of my singing career was serving at my church. I had loved my work, picking just the right songs to complement the theme for the Sunday Mass and leading the congregation in singing them. At times when we sang together the air would become still, signaling to me a tangible presence of the Holy Spirit. Now, all of a sudden, something I loved doing had become terrifying. I never knew if or when my voice would "show up for work."

The doctor had prescribed treatment with medication, dietary changes, and vocal rest. The road back to a restored voice would be long and difficult with no guarantees. I began to wonder if the work involved would be worth it. While I was upset that my voice had gotten so weak, I was surprised at how ready I was to let it go.

The deaths of my parents over the past seven years had taken their toll. My lifelong passion was dying as a result. With little desire and energy to rehab my music career, I eventually decided to put it aside. I continued to sing in church, but it took on a perfunctory quality. There was little resolve left when my voice began to fail.

We lose loved ones, and we lose ourselves in the process. We can be struck with illnesses and ailments that restrict our capabilities. We age and face the reality of our growing limitations. It was a time of dancing, and now it is a time of mourning, to paraphrase Ecclesiastes 3:4. Key questions come to mind: What is it like to lose such a large part of yourself? How do you cope after spending a lifetime pouring yourself into your passion?

I think of star athletes who, as they approach the age of forty, must come to grips with losing their abilities. New England Patriots linebacker Tedy Bruschi was nearly forced to retire at age thirty two because of a stroke. Lying in his hospital bed and suffering from partial paralysis, what must he have been thinking? Football was everything to him, and at the height of his career, in the prime of life, it appeared to be over. Ultimately he was able to fight his way back and play an additional four years before retiring at age thirty six.[1] He was granted the grace of those four years to process the idea of retirement and make plans to move on, but even with that preparation, it was the death of something he had held dear his whole life. How must he have felt?

Julie Andrews was open in sharing how she felt about losing her singing voice after a botched throat operation. That iconic pure soprano, a voice beloved by millions because of her roles as Maria von Trapp and Mary Poppins, was gone forever. She compared losing her voice to a death. Her stepdaughter Jennifer Edwards remarked that, when her stepmother lost her voice, she lost her identity.[2]

Eventually we face the prospect of letting go of something we cherish about ourselves. As my voice began to lose consistency, I knew how others felt: the loss of my voice truly was a death. I missed that sensual feeling of singing, how it used to vibrate in my throat and buzz in my head. I'd never again hear that nice clear sound echo throughout the church and come back to me. I had sung with such ease that I could forget all about the technique of singing and just get into the prayer of it. There were times when those memories would flood my mind, and I would break out in spontaneous tears.

After months of trying to make it work, I finally decided to resign from the parish music ministry. Leaving was not easy. My resignation meant that the other musicians, especially the music director, had to pick up the slack. I felt guilty. And, at the same time, I felt angry and frustrated at the difficulty of explaining to others that I could no longer sing. Some didn't believe me. The pain of my loss hit me with such deliberate force that I began to push music away.

It was that challenge described in Ecclesiastes 3 playing itself out. I wanted to refrain from embracing my music. I wanted to tear it down. I wanted to kill it.

Flow Lesson 6

Resistance

Materials needed: computer or tablet, a piece of furniture or a heavy object, a pen or pencil and paper

Before beginning this exercise, take a few moments to be still using some of the techniques in previous exercises and sense the presence of God within you. Ask the Holy Spirit to guide you through this activity and reveal what he wants you to know.

Next, find something in your house that is difficult to move, such as a piece of furniture. Don't decide on something that you cannot move at all. Preferably it would be on a smooth surface such as a wood floor. Stand in front of that object and imagine the following. The object will represent a loss you may not be ready to accept. Pulling the object toward you means that you accept your loss. Pushing it away means you do not accept it. The surface upon which the object stands represents God's grace, holding your loss.

Link your loss to the object and try pushing it away. You need not push it hard; you only want to get a sense of the resistance. Think about what you are feeling as you push. Now stop pushing, and write down what just happened. Try connecting the physical sense of pushing the object with how you are feeling with your loss. If you are having trouble making that connection, first make a list of single words describing what it was like to push the object and feel the resistance. Now, in a separate column, write down single words that describe how you feel about what you have lost and how you feel when people seek to console you. Do you feel that same resistance? How does it play out in your life? How do you feel about your resistance? Do you feel connected to God in your loss? If you do not feel a connection with God, what do you feel? Feel free to write down anything you wish, even if it denotes anger, resentment, frustration, or a loss of faith. This is your own private time between yourself and God, and he already knows how you feel.

Next, pull the object gently toward you and think about what you are feeling as you pull. Now stop pulling and write down your impressions. Was it easier to pull the object toward you or to push it away? Try making a connection to your loss: Right now, is it harder to pull that loss toward you or to push it away? Why?

Finally, imagine that someone is with you (or you might even invite someone to be with you during this exercise) and that, while you were pulling on the object, they were pushing. How do you feel physically now that you have help? How much easier would it be to pull the object forward if you had help? Who does your help represent?

Watch the video of Paul McCartney's song "Tug of War" (visit beasone.org, click on the "Resources" tab and then "Flow Lesson 6" to find this video) to spark further ideas and impressions.

Go back now and read Ecclesiastes 3:1–8. In light of what you just did, write down your impressions of the verses. What do they mean to you now? How do you feel about that area of your life that you have been trying to push away? How does the cyclical nature of life, as described in Ecclesiastes, make you feel? Write or speak a prayer to God to help you understand your feelings.

Hiding in Christ

In my confusion and guilt I turned to the scriptures and found myself sympathizing with the disciple Thomas as depicted in John 20:24–29. When the others told him that they had "seen the Lord," he refused to believe. He treated their story with skepticism that bordered on rejection. He was provocative in his declaration that he would not believe unless he placed his hand in the side of Jesus and probed the wounds with his fingers.[3] Thomas deliberately pushed away any semblance of hope that Jesus was alive. He did not dare to believe. Reading that passage, I understood the bitterness in his demands and the refusal to face his pain. When Jesus appeared to all the apostles several days later, he invited Thomas to do as the others had done: touch his wounds.

There was a beautiful homily delivered at the Basilica of the Sacred Heart at the University of Notre Dame by Rev. Patrick Reidy, C.S.C., on this gospel passage. Newly ordained, it was Fr. Reidy's first public celebration of the liturgy. He imagined Jesus ministering to Thomas in this way: "'Put your finger here and see my hands. Bring your hand and put it into my side. Hide yourself in me. Hide yourself from all that troubles you, all you doubt, from all you fear. Hide yourself in a love more penetrating than a brush fire, more overwhelming than a deluge. Hide your-self in a love that will remake you entirely. Do not be afraid.'"[4]

Thomas was invited to "touch resurrection, to touch eternity." He was transformed by the Lord's lavish show of love, causing a total change of heart in the man who then called Jesus "my Lord and my God" with an amazing confession of faith.[5]

We too have the ability to meet the Lord and to hide ourselves in him as Thomas did because of the Eucharist. Since as Catholics we believe the Eucharist truly is the Body and Blood of Christ; since it resides in tabernacles across the world waiting for us to come, sit, and adore; and since we can ingest the Eucharist so that it courses through our veins, we too can "touch resurrection, touch eternity." Vinny Flynn in *7 Secrets of the Eucharist* states, "The Eucharist is not a thing. It is not a dead object. It is Christ, and he is *fully alive*. Receiving Him with this awareness, we become more fully alive."[6] As a quotation from Pope John Paul II reads, "The flesh of the Son of Man, given as food, is his body in its glorious state after the resurrection."[7] Jesus was in this same state when he encouraged Thomas to touch his wounds. Hidden in the Eucharist, Christ is only waiting for us to come to him, to ask to receive him, to request a hiding place within him.

The Eucharist is so easily accessible to me that I had forgotten Jesus was there. I realize now that, had I accepted that invitation to "touch resurrection, touch eternity," I would have better understood why I wanted to push away my pain. The entitlement I felt to grieve alone was pride, erecting a wall that I could not get through on my own.

I am reminded of my friend Reg, who has much that she could have been bitter about. Once an avid reader who prided herself on her organization skills, she could no longer concentrate long enough to finish anything. During the birth of her fourth child, she was rushed into intensive care with a rare complication that nearly took her life. The result was that her brain was robbed of oxygen, which left her impaired. Not only did it make it impossible for her to read but also to follow sequences and correlate.[8] The medical complication also resulted in a devastating physical loss: she could not have any more children. She cried over that loss for ten years.[9]

I have known Reg since high school and remember well what she was like before the change. She was the epitome of focus, efficiency, and competence. To hear her describe herself as distracted and scatterbrained, driving people crazy with her fidgety ways, didn't sound like my friend at all. Reg fought against her mental disabilities with great frustration, railing against God while appealing for help as well. She and her family appeared perfect to those around them who only saw the well-scrubbed outside; inside she was resentful that people dismissed her suffering so easily.[10]

God answered her appeals but not by restoring her mental capacities. Instead he offered her the example of Moses. Asked by the Lord to lead the Israelites out of Egypt, he at first resisted God's request, describing himself as "slow of speech and slow of tongue" (Ex 4:10). Moses further resisted because he was just one man. He had no army, no weapons, no means of freeing the Israelites except for his shepherd's staff and his perceived lack of eloquence. Moses chose to trust in God; that trust resulted in the breaking of Pharaoh's will and the leading of the Israelites out of the bondage of Egypt to the Promised Land.

Moses tapped into the flow of grace by trusting in God; that ensuing partnership produced creative solutions that made use of Moses's weakness and his trust rather than armies and weapons. God transformed Moses from a man in exile, "slow of speech and slow of tongue," to one of the greatest leaders of the Jewish people. He was used by God to transform a nation.

Reg sensed an invitation from God to do the same, giving over her brokenness to him ("a beat-up body and a leaky mind"[11]) and trusting in him to put her to good use despite her limitations. And he has. Despite her "leaky mind," Reg shares her creative writing talents as an award-winning columnist for *The Catholic Transcript*. Her work has appeared in many other publications. She assembled her best columns into a book, *Do Bad Guys Wear Socks?*, despite the organizational nightmare that assembling such a book presented. In it she shares her unique brand of humor, gritty reality, and spiritual insight woven through stories taken from her life with her husband and four children. Just as God successfully used Moses with all his limitations to appeal to Pharaoh for the release of the Israelites, he is using Reg, "leaky mind" and all, to bless many through her writing and her life.

Thomas could not face his bitterness until he encountered Jesus himself. The result was the Lord meeting Thomas exactly where he was and graciously granting him what he needed to overcome his pain. The Lord met Reg where she was, frustrated over her loss, and granted her the grace to trust him and thus work through her limitations. All of us who build a protective casing through bitterness and fear call out (sometimes quietly, desperately) for a similar encounter. I had to learn, like Thomas and Reg, to acknowledge that need. I had to find out what was blinding me.

Yielding to the Current

The grieving process provided the way. I became acutely aware that my singing was something that was built through community; yet, I insisted upon mourning in private. Daniel B. Hinshaw, MD, an Orthodox Christian and a practicing physician, writes of suffering in the context of community: how the constriction of a person's role due to infirmity acts as a ripple effect across the community.[12] It was that ripple effect that I began to see. I could no longer fulfill my obligations, which affected the workload of my fellow musicians. Parishioners missed my singing, offering their condolences and their hopes that my voice would be restored one day.

It appeared that Thomas kept his grief over Jesus' crucifixion close to his heart, out of view of the others, perhaps because it was too raw to share. Sometimes when pain is that deep, any reminder of it, even if it is manifested in kind words and gestures, is too much to take. Rather than being comforted by the kindness of my parish community, I found it to be intrusive. In an effort to protect myself from further pain, my grief had created a wall that prevented real healing.

Gifts properly shared are communal; this is not limited to famous performers and athletes. Perhaps you are someone in your church or community who for years has faithfully led a group or committee, cooked meals week after week for soup kitchens, taught religious education, or sung every Sunday in the choir. You likely gave it everything you had, and people came to depend on you. Your gifts of leadership, organization, teaching, cooking, or music were sorely missed when you decided it was time to walk away. Having invested so much of yourself into the work, you might wonder, "How will I feel when I leave this work behind? What does that mean for those I served? How might they respond and how will I feel about that?"

I know how I felt: I wanted nothing more to do with my old life. I began to convince myself that music meant nothing to me just so I could push away the pain of the loss. My life was moving in a different direction with new interests, and I wanted to go with that flow, unimpeded. With denial came a spirit of ingratitude and a lack of graciousness. I gritted my teeth and fought hard to put on a pleasant face each time someone mentioned my music or when I heard music that I formerly would

have been involved with at my church. In truth, I deeply resented
the intrusion and the constant reminder of my pain.

In choosing to fight the elements rather than yielding to
them, I was cutting out a large portion of my life. And yet,
throughout this pushing away, I sensed a small voice whispering,
"Reconcile." Reconcile? What did that mean? I felt entitled to
grieve alone, and therein lay the problem.

In order for reconciliation to come, I had to acknowledge
that my singing voice was on loan. All of our gifts and talents
are on loan. *Everything* belongs to God, the Creator of everyone
and everything: parents, children, friends, the things we do, the
way we think, the bodies we inhabit. As Job cried out, "The
Lord gave, and the Lord has taken away; blessed be the name of
the Lord." Job understood his place in the universe: "Naked I
came from my mother's womb, and naked shall I return there"
(Jb 1:21). He knew he was entitled to nothing but was subject
to God's love and mercy. It did not mean that he didn't grieve,
for he did, having lost his livelihood, family, and eventually his
health. Job was to discover through an intervention from God
himself that the Lord's way of thinking was beyond his understanding, and that acceptance of his will, whether Job understood it or not, was the only path to healing. I too had to place
my trust in God even though I did not as yet understand.

Our gifts and talents provide opportunities to show our
love for each other. God gave us these things precisely to share,
and if we have done that well, others will miss them when we
can no longer offer them. Anyone who has taken care of sick,
elderly parents knows that, yearning for the days when they
took care of us. Mom, with her delicious home-cooked meals
and the way she'd nurse us when we were sick. Dad, giving wise
counsel and standing up for us when were in trouble. Their care
for us was a sharing of their various gifts and talents. They grieve

because they can no longer give as they used to, and we grieve for those lost days.

I was ashamed of my ingratitude and impatience toward those who had enjoyed my singing and supported me over the years. It revealed an ugly underbelly: Just how much love was involved in sharing my gift, and how much of it was commandeered by my pride?

Performers are known for their egos, and I certainly had mine. It made me possessive of my gift. I was just like the toddler who gets a toy for her birthday. She rips off the wrapping paper and squeals with glee over her new toy, possibly forgetting to thank her parents for it. She may hug it. She *will* cling to it. She will carry it with her everywhere, and if her brother tries to take it away from her, she will clutch it closer to her chest, never intending to share. She may clutch it so hard that she ends up breaking the beloved toy.

This is how I treated my gift of music. I clutched it close to me just like that child. I shared it only as it suited my purposes. Taking my gift for granted, I did not take proper care of it. Music came so easily to me that I never thought I had to work at improving my craft. I came to the stark realization that I had never once actually prayed to God about it; never once did I ask him to bless it or protect it, nor did I ask for the grace and guidance to take care of my gift and use it properly.

Pride in *my* music. *My* songs. *My* voice. Just like the toddler with the toy. I had failed to grasp the most basic concept: my gift was on loan. It did not belong to me, and it would not last forever. How well had I used this precious gift?

Pride did not end when my voice went away. It disguised itself as "stoicism" and "courage." In public I accepted my loss quickly and with grace. In actuality I was running away from my loss. Condolences and inquiries from family and friends felt like an intrusion because they were forcing me to look at the pain of loss. The reality was that my pride was responsible for muddying the waters, thus stoking the anger, frustration, and impatience. It was the block to the reconciliation that God desired.

This grief journey could have ended in bitterness and regret; but instead, God, in his infinite goodness showed great mercy, leading me to reconciliation, joy, and a second chance. After nearly four years of fighting the current, I decided to obey, taking my first tentative steps in the other direction. I had no idea where I was going or where it would lead or if I even wanted to go there at all. Accepting the invitation from God to reconcile was Ecclesiastes 3 playing out again but in the opposite way. Instead of killing, there would now be healing. Instead of tearing down, building. Although my voice was not what it was, I was still being prepared to embrace my music again with loving arms. I could never have guessed just how far he would take me.

Flow Lesson 7

Illustrating the Cycle of Life

Materials needed: computer or tablet; pen or pencil and paper; crayons, colored pencils, or colored chalk; bible

Before beginning this exercise, take a few moments to be still using one or more of the techniques from previous exercises, and sense the presence of God within you. Ask the Holy Spirit to guide you through this activity and reveal what he wants you to know.

Fold the paper in half first vertically, and then in half horizontally. Draw a circle such that both folds run through the center of the circle. Choose a verse from Ecclesiastes 3:1–8, such as "a time to mourn and a time to dance"; on the left side of the circle on the horizontal fold, write the first part of the verse (i.e., "a time to mourn"), and on the opposite side, write the other half of the verse ("a time to dance").

Choose colors from your pencils, crayons, or chalk that represent how you feel about the first half of the verse, and then choose colors to express how you feel about the second half.

Begin coloring in the circle, starting from the upper, left-hand side at the fold—the idea is that the colors will eventually change from the colors associated with mourning to colors associated with dancing. Blend the colors together to create different shades, or simply press down hard with the crayon, chalk, or pencil to achieve a darker color, and press down gently for a lighter color.

Complete the top half circle and examine it for a few moments, perhaps talking to God about what you see. Now finish the lower part of the circle, working from the right back to the left; the colors will represent going from dancing back to mourning. Feel free, if you wish, to choose different colors for this half of the circle, so long as they represent your feelings toward dancing and mourning.

Once the circle is completely colored in, reflect upon your life, and write down one or two times when you were more attuned to the left-hand side of the circle; now do the same for the right-hand side. How does the shape of the circle and how it has been colored inspire hope? How does it relate to the verse you chose from Ecclesiastes 3?

Go back to those times you listed that were more attuned to the left-hand side of the circle and consider their resolution. Write a letter to God or simply talk with him about how that difficult time moved to some sort of resolution. What did grace have to do with that resolution? Was there a healing or a correction of the problem? Did you instead learn to make peace with that time in your life even though it might not have been resolved as you would have liked? Once you are through describing this period in your life, take some time to be quiet so that you can sense his reply.

Finally, watch the following two videos (Visit beasone. org, click "Resource" tab and then "Flow Lesson 7" to find these videos.):

1. "Circle Game" by Joni Mitchell, (about the cyclical nature of life) sung when she was young.

2. "Both Sides Now" by Joni Mitchell (about seeing different sides to clouds, life, and love), sung when she was much older.

Note the change of mood and voice—can you sense how the cycles of life have affected this artist? Do you feel any similarity between your own experience and what you detect in her singing of these songs? How has your faith in God sustained you through the different cycles of your life?

Entering the Flow

That first small step back to music was taken with my high school Confirmation class. After hearing a speaker who had worked with Mother Teresa, we returned to our classrooms to discuss it. Since music has a unique way of conveying a message, I wanted to present the right song to the class that would affirm what we had learned about Mother Teresa's mission, while creating an atmosphere conducive to prayer and reflection. Searching through my iPod, I came upon one of my own songs called "Teach Me to Love." The words were perfect, but the song was recorded in a way that would not produce the ambiance I desired. I paused, wondering if I still had the voice to sing it live in front of my students. Singing to them in person would create a sense of intimacy that a recording could never achieve. I decided to go for it. I loved these kids and wanted to give them the best opportunity for meaningful prayer and reflection. The result was that sweet stillness in the air followed by spontaneous applause. By overcoming fear, I was able to lead my students into a sacred moment. I gave, the gift was returned, and it became a prayer.

The memory of that moment lingered in my mind as I prepared for the Confirmation retreat the following weekend. The woman who normally provided the live music could not be with us. There were several songs that she sang at certain moments during the retreat that I felt were essential. Could I perform them? Sensing an invitation from within, I decided to step out in faith.

While singing at the retreat, I began to realize there was much more to my music than just singing, playing the guitar, and writing songs. There were the more than two decades of experience, a deep well that I could draw upon to compensate for my lack of voice. I thought back to when I had seen Rosemary Clooney, one of my favorite singers, perform live. She was in her seventies when I saw her. With a weathered voice she drew upon her own deep well to present a beautiful performance. She had made peace with her limitations and exuded a quiet confidence, guiding the audience past any physical limitations into an experience of the song. Could I share from a deep well, too?

I opted to try. During the retreat I gave myself over to the songs and their meaning. I remembered the lesson of Clooney and used her technique. As I lost myself in the music, *letting go* lifted me above my physical limitations. My desire to serve the Confirmation students, *my love for them*, gave me the courage to step out of the way and let God do his work. I began to see singing in a different way, as something to be given away rather than "owned" and controlled.

Finally after the long battle I said yes to God, entering into his flow, allowing his river of grace to carry me. Each invitation to sing was an opportunity to stop fighting, to stop trying to manage my grief on my own, and to be reconciled to this part of myself. It was Jesus, coming to me as he came to Thomas. He did not judge nor chastise Thomas for his provocative challenge but rather gave him the opportunity to face his grief, work through it, and accept healing and transformation. I was given the same opportunity. Rather than being mired in my narrow perception of what I had lost, I could begin to appreciate what I still had in a new light.

Stepping out can be both frightening and empowering. We hesitate in fear even though that quiet voice inside is saying, "Go for it!" We're taking a leap off a mountain, hoping, trusting, that we won't crash. Thomas wouldn't believe because he was afraid to crash; that first blow, the death of his Lord, had been a crushing experience. I was afraid to sing in public because of previous times when my voice had failed, and I had felt morti-fied. Perhaps you are afraid to crash for fear of being hurt again. The good news is that Jesus is as close to us as our breath; we can receive him in the Eucharist daily if we want to. The Lord never leaves our side or our heart, even if we can't perceive him. The hand of God is always ready to support us, steady us, lead us to where we need to go, even if we need to wade into grace's rushing current. The love that we have for others is the catalyst. It's all just a matter of taking that first step in trust.

This was just the beginning of the healing. Several months after the retreat, I had my throat blessed on the feast of St. Blaise. The wait was long, giving me time to reflect. Did I want my voice to be healed? Did I believe healing was possible? I didn't even know why I was there. Little did I know the many graces that would come from accepting God's latest invitation.

A few days later my son started asking me about the collection of songs I had written long ago. He is a songwriter as well, playing in a band and recording. He knew I had written those songs when I was his age, and he wanted me to send them to him. I pulled out the cassettes and started listening. The songs sounded better than I had originally thought. Slowly I began to remember why I had fallen in love with music in the first place. I sent him the songs, and he listened. This led to many wonderful conversations about music, and it felt like a soothing balm. Listening to my old songs, reliving the memories, and then sharing all of this with my son began the process of reconciliation.

Instead of being raw and fragmented, I began to feel whole. A sense of wonder and deep gratitude welled up inside. The following Sunday as I entered the church to go to Mass, I was immediately struck with the knowledge that I had received a significant healing with that throat blessing. I couldn't wait to tell the priest.

Thereafter during Mass I noticed that it became easier to sing the hymns. Buoyed, I pushed my voice a bit further each week. One day while driving home after Mass, I sang some of the most challenging songs in my repertoire, including "I Know That My Redeemer Liveth" from Handel's *Messiah,* and discovered to my delight that I could sing them just as I had before. My voice had been restored. I had received a physical healing along with an emotional and spiritual healing.

Fear had silenced my voice more than the physical ailments; I could not bear to sing in public again, afraid that my voice would fail. Accepting those small invitations from God, stepping out in faith, through all those little yeses, I was able to turn around. Tearing down and pushing away turned to embracing, reconciliation, and healing. It did not happen as one major act but as a culmination, of many small steps, gradually turning around to God's will. I was beginning to flow with the current.

Healing of the Whole

Because of the manner in which my voice was restored, I am compelled to wonder if there was a connection between the loss of my voice and my mother's death. A quick search on the internet about GERD revealed that stress indeed can have some effect on acid reflux. Healthline.com cites research suggesting that persons under stress are more sensitive to pain and thus more acutely feel the effects of heartburn.[13]

While I have no solid evidence of any relationship between the onslaught of GERD and my mother's illness and death, I still consider the possibility. Unable to express any sadness at the time of her death as a result of being in "battle mode" from taking care of her, could my body have been expressing it for me? It took about a year for that numbness to melt away, while at the same time I was pushing away the pain of losing my voice. In some shape or form, such strong feelings will express themselves. If we are not willing to meet them head on, deeply rooted feelings will find other ways to vent.

In reflecting upon the healing of my voice, I know that the emotional component was the key to the physical manifestation. In fact, I believe the physical could not have happened had I not worked through my feelings regarding music. Not only did the blessing that day strengthen my vocal cords; it opened my heart to embracing music again. This would explain why with each succeeding week my voice grew stronger as I sang the hymns at

Mass—and why the emotional connection to music, the love, was renewed.

As a result, I have learned that healing is so much more than a cure of the physical symptoms; it is the restoration of the whole person. And while the physical portion may happen in an instance, the true healing of the interior person unfolds over time. That unfolding requires our partnership with the Great Physician; we must take the medicine and perform the disciplines necessary to retain that healing and grow from it. I still have many issues to work through regarding my music, including that newfound fear to perform in public and working through my writer's block regarding songwriting. As one who has been healed, I have a responsibility to follow through, seeing that healing to its fruition.

Just as I had experienced during our financial troubles, as we continue to say yes to God, the blessings will multiply. I think of the story of the handful of loaves and fishes feeding five thousand from Matthew's gospel. Jesus invited his disciples to feed the people, but they resisted. "We have nothing here but five loaves and two fish," they said (Mt 14:17). Jesus accepted the small amount of food, everything the disciples and the people had to offer, and multiplied it to feed five thousand people.

This is what we witness each time we accept an invitation from God to give of ourselves: the blessings multiply exponentially. Again I was experiencing "a good measure, pressed down, shaken together, running over," just as Jesus had promised (Lk 6:38). For me it was not just the ability to sing to my students but the fact that I received back the ability to pray. I learned at last how to show my love to others through my singing. I didn't just receive an emotional healing from having my throat blessed; I received a *complete* healing of body, heart, mind, and soul—all because I chose to leave myself open to whatever God wanted to do.

Healing, however, does not happen in a vacuum; it happens within a community. Had I not agreed to have my throat blessed by the priest, there would have been no healing. Had I not shared my songs with my son, I would have missed the opportunity for emotional healing. Had I decided that singing along with the congregation each week at Mass was too difficult, too painful, I would never have discovered that my voice was, in fact, getting stronger.

All this came to mind when I heard the gospel reading at Mass one Sunday. The priest read from John 11:1–45 about the raising of Lazarus from the dead. When he got to the part where Jesus asked that the stone be removed from the tomb, I realized my stone had been my pride. It had locked me in a tomb of my own making. The only way to have the stone removed and emerge from that tomb was to put aside my pride and reach out to others by giving of myself, whether I felt ready or not. Like Lazarus, I became unbound, not by my own efforts but because I chose to place myself in God's flow of grace, sharing myself with others even when it involved the risk of facing my pain and grief head-on.

In the echoes of Ecclesiastes 3, we can turn from killing to healing, from tearing down to building up, from refraining to embracing. From fighting the current to letting God lead us home, we can learn to float on the river of grace, on the path that leads to wholeness again.

Questions for Reflection

1. Have you suffered a loss of function in your body or lost the ability to do something you loved doing? If so, what function have you lost? How did you lose that function or ability? Was

it sudden or over a period of time? What was your initial reaction? How do you feel now?

2. Are you aware of some pain, trauma, or unhappy memory in your life that you are unable to face, and if so, what is it? Why don't you want to face it? What do you think would happen if you did try to face it, knowing that Jesus was at your side?

3. Are you someone who suffers privately, in silence, while appearing to be "fine" to those around you? What prompts you to hide your suffering? How do you feel when people don't take your suffering seriously? What steps could you take to reconcile your private suffering with your public persona?

4. In the midst of a trial or deep mourning, have you ever felt entitled to suffer alone? When people are kind to you and offer help, what is your reaction? If you fail to derive consolation from them, why do you think that happens? If Jesus were to appear in bodily form before you, what would you say to him about your pain?

5. Have you been heavily invested in your career, hobby, or volunteer effort and now find yourself having to give it up because of having children, health reasons, retirement, being laid off, or being replaced? How do you feel about this change? If you are experiencing resistance or bitterness and are unable to reconcile your feelings, what steps can you take to bring your concerns before the Lord?

6. Upon sensing an invitation from God to do something that unnerves you, how did you feel? What was that invitation and how did you act upon it? If you feel unable to accept the invitation, what steps can you take to tap into the power of God's grace to overcome your resistance?

Visit beasone.org, click on the "Resources" tab and then "Flow Lessons" for additional activities to facilitate a deeper exploration of the concepts of this chapter. Videos, music, and examples are supplied to help you with these exercises.

Chapter 4—Exploring New Tributaries

What Louisa May Alcott Taught Me about Beginning Anew

I love to explore when I go kayaking, and I always find something new. Coves and hideaway spaces are favorites on the pond, and tributaries take me deeper into the heart of the river. The possibilities of encountering a stiff current, unfamiliar terrain, and loss of direction all cross my mind when I discover a tributary, but curiosity wins out. Returning from such trips, I feel peaceful and satisfied.

The grief process opens tributaries that beckon us deep within. Its flow can be stronger than we'd like, leading us through a path of twists and turns. We look for familiar landmarks to cling to and often feel lost. We could be in danger of becoming mired in the mud. Realizing after a while that paddling against the current is a futile effort, we give in to its relentless drive to move forward. The question is, do we look at this journey as fruitless and leading to despair or as a new beginning leading to healing and discovery?

My grief journey has lasted more than ten years. Ten years of illness and death: my father's swift and horrific, and my mother's lingering and full of despair. Losing my voice added an additional murky layer. It had left me numb and unable to cry.

The death of a loved one is life changing; there is no getting around it. The experience of grief is as varied as the people it affects. It's our autobiography with our name stamped on the cover. Our story could be engulfed in sadness; we may be unable to move, incapable of accepting what has happened. Our story could be filled with anger, railing at life, at people, at God for the injustice of taking our loved one (especially if that person was young or the death sudden). In our story, we could be feeling nothing. Perhaps we appear not to be grieving until suddenly it pours out of us years after the loss. My story was definitely not what I imagined it would be.

In *Praying Our Goodbyes*, Joyce Rupp writes how our "one-liners" can define who we are and how we will react to life. What are your "one-liners"? Mine are these: "There is a solution to every problem," and, "I'm slow but I get it eventually." Both one-liners played out to perfection during my time of mourning: I looked at grief as a problem to be solved; yet at the same time, I was slow to grasp what was really happening. All I knew was that each time I experienced a loss I was filled with energy rather than drained, and this surprised me. Has grief ever compelled you to act out, to do something? Did you feel a need to clear out the family home immediately after your mother or father died? Did you put things away so as not to be reminded, or did you take every memento you could and surround yourself with memories for fear you would forget your loved one?

In my case it was the compulsion to rearrange space. When my father died, I spearheaded the purchase of our house, thus completely changing our living space. When I lost my singing voice, I moved anything music related into the basement. When my mother passed away, we prepared the family home for sale.

I worked with the realtor while my sister took care of the renovations, and the home was sold a mere month after my mother died.

Grief acted as a teacher, showing me a part of myself I never knew existed. Having prided myself on self-knowledge, I found this quite humbling. Obviously I had a lot more to learn. New tributaries were opening up, and I did not resist. The tributary I chose to explore after losing my mother and my voice started innocently enough but blossomed over time, transforming my life.

It began with a thoughtful gift from my husband. Rich had bought a couple of books for me during the last year of my mother's illness, both related to Louisa May Alcott. Aware of my longstanding interest in Louisa, he thought that reading might ease the pain. I hadn't had the heart to read them while my mother was sick, but after she died I was ready for something new.

Normally I did not read much. The one exception was a curious ritual that played out every few years: I would read a biography of Louisa May Alcott and then visit Orchard House, the family homestead that is now a museum in Concord, Massachusetts, not far from where I live. Each time I could feel the spirit of Louisa and her sisters in the house while I secretly touched Louisa's (Jo's) small desk where *Little Women* was written, gazing upon Anna's (Meg's) gray silk wedding dress made by the bride herself, "hearing" strains of music from Elizabeth's (Beth's) melodeon, and admiring the many sketches and paintings done directly on the walls of the house by youngest sister May (Amy).

Louisa had captured my imagination as a girl. I was introduced to her through a story of her life given to me by my aunt. I felt a kindred spirit with the tomboy who put on plays with her sisters in the family barn, struggled with a bad temper, wrote stories in the apple tree, and longed for a room of her own. As an adult I identified with Louisa's severe mood swings and how she lost herself in her writing, falling into what she called her "vortex." Having experienced many of these things myself, I found that reading about Louisa helped me to understand myself a bit better.

It made sense then to turn to Louisa again for comfort and guidance. I started with the historical novel, thinking it would make for an entertaining read. *The Lost Summer of Louisa May Alcott* by Kelly O'Connor McNees is a "what if" story: What if Louisa, who in real life never married, had experienced a passionate summer romance? I was lost in the book in an instant, carried away to nineteenth-century New Hampshire where handsome Joseph Singer courted a stubborn Louisa until she eventually succumbed to his charms.

Around this time Rich alerted me to a PBS documentary about Louisa. It was the first time such a movie had been made, and I was excited at the prospect of "seeing" Louisa on the screen. The program was called *Louisa May Alcott: The Woman Behind Little Women*, based upon the biography by Harriet Reisen; ironically, this was the second book Rich had bought for me.

Having just finished *Lost Summer*, I dove headlong into *Louisa May Alcott: The Woman Behind Little Women*. The author's thorough knowledge of and deep passion for Louisa's canon inspired me to read Louisa's own words for the first time. It began not with *Little Women* but with *Hospital Sketches*, a thinly veiled memoir of her experience as a Civil War nurse. Her moving description of the death of a virtuous soldier named John Suhre and how she had nursed him acted as a soothing balm on my grief. She described death as noble, and her belief in the afterlife was unmistakable. Where once I had felt a kinship with Louisa because of our mutually shared mood swings, deep tempers, and passions for our art, now I identified with the woman who found sacredness and hope in death just as I had. While Louisa wrote mainly to support her family, it seemed that the act of creating helped her to work through her own grief after the tragic passing of her younger sister Elizabeth, whom she called her "conscience" and "spiritual guide."

Harriet Reisen's book proved to be life changing. I could not just finish the book and be done with it, as in the past. This time I opted to reach out. I contacted Reisen with thoughts about her book, and we ended up conversing for more than an hour on the phone. It was the first time I had ever had the chance to share my passion about Louisa with someone; I appreciated her kindness in indulging a perfect stranger.

Fueled by that conversation, I decided to search on the Internet for a blog or a website where the conversation could continue. Despite many websites with information about the Alcott family, there was no place where interaction could take place. It was then that I decided to create my own blog in the hopes of attracting and building a community of Alcott enthusiasts. I called it *Louisa May Alcott Is My Passion*. Soon a small and vibrant community sprung up around the blog.

I knew my mother had enjoyed Louisa May Alcott's books; her collection contained several titles. Thumbing through her copy of *Little Women* marked with her personal nameplate, I could feel her presence inside of me. In my mind we turned the pages together, horrified over Amy's dastardly deed of burning Jo's manuscript; laughing over the escapades of the sisters with Laurie, the boy next door; incensed over the injustice of Amy's winning the trip to Europe with Aunt March when it had been promised to Jo; shocked and saddened by Jo's rejection of Laurie; crying copious tears over the passing of sweet Beth. It made me feel close to my mother again.

Reading Louisa's books, writing about them on the blog, and talking about them with my new online friends filled a gaping hole in my life. The numbing effect of grief began to melt away; slowly, memories emerged of the vital and caring woman who had been my mother: the woman with an insatiable curiosity, a passion for learning, a zest for life, and a love that knew no bounds. Her legacy started to come alive in me.

In the back of my mind, however, I wondered why I still did not cry or feel sad over losing my mother because I had cherished her. I felt uncertain about, even embarrassed by, my lack of sadness. My sister and brother would call to share their feelings, and I had a difficult time responding to them. I didn't want to appear unaffected by my mother's death, for I was; I just didn't know yet how I was affected. Grief had me completely baffled; I was beginning to think something was wrong with me.

Flow Lesson 8

The River and Its Tributaries

Materials needed: computer or tablet, loose sand or dirt, large square or rectangular Tupperware container, water

Before beginning this exercise, take a few moments to be still and sense the presence of God within you. Ask the Holy Spirit to guide you through this activity and reveal what he wants you to know.

Search for images on your computer using the phrase "river with tributaries." (If you don't have access to a computer, try going to the library or a bookstore to search for a picture of a river with tributaries). After choosing an image to examine, take your finger and trace the different branches of the river. Write down a brief description of what you see.

Next, take a large rectangular or square Tupperware container and fill it halfway with loose dirt or sand. Make sure the dirt or sand is moistened such that you can mold and shape it. Create some hills and valleys with your dirt or sand. Next, using three fingers together, create a wide, curving path symbolizing a river. Once done, create several smaller branches or tributaries with one finger. When you have created your river and tributaries, take a small amount of water and slowly fill the main river path, watching the water filling in the branches; you may need to adjust the amount of water you use or tilt the container to make all the branches fill with water. Write down a brief description of what you see, especially how the water moves over the hills and valleys you created.

Now read the following passage from Ezekiel, praying for insight from the Holy Spirit:

> Wherever the river goes, every living creature that swarms will live, and there will be very many fish, once these waters reach there. It will become fresh; and everything will live where the river goes. . . . On the banks, on both sides of the river, there will grow all kinds of trees for food. Their leaves will not wither nor their fruit fail, but they will bear fresh fruit every month, because the water for them flows from the sanctuary. Their fruit will be for food, and their leaves for healing. (Ez 47:9, 12)

Look again at your river and tributaries and reflect on these verses. What does the main river represent to you? What do the branches represent? Image that this river and its tributaries describe your life. What story does it tell? Reflecting on a recent

part of your life, write down your experiences using the imagery
of the river and the tributaries in your description.

Take this exercise a step further by going outside and gathering small green leaves and plants and placing them in your
container to illustrate these verses. What good things have come
into your life as a result of your relationship to the main river
and its tributaries?

Watch the video of "River of Grace" by Matthew Baute.
Imagine where grace has taken you in your life, thinking of
specific episodes; write them down. Include both the good and
difficult times in your life as they come to you. After the song
ends, look over your list and offer a prayer of thanksgiving to
God for each episode. Visit beasone.org, click on the "Resource"
tab and then "Flow Lesson 8" to find this video.

Allowing Myself to Be Changed

The scriptures are filled with references to grief, many of them
directed toward comforting the mourner. Revelation 21:4 says,
"He will wipe every tear from their eyes. Death will be no more;
mourning and crying and pain will be no more, for the first
things have passed away." This passage is usually interpreted
to mean that these things will happen after we reach heaven
with the perfection of eternal life. Yet I was experiencing these
things now. My faith in the afterlife and my trust in God's mercy
toward my parents were unshakable, sustaining me through the
loss. I attended our parish's bereavement group and listened to
people describing their crises of faith and how they found it
nearly impossible to pray or attend Mass. How could I share that
the opposite was true for me? Was I dishonoring their grief by

talking about the blessing God had given me to fill the vacuum? Was it right to keep these feelings to myself?

I was finding grief to be as mysterious as death. Like death, it is something that cannot be controlled, something that will inevitably require our submission. But like everything else we face in life, we can decide how to react to it. Will we allow ourselves to go on the journey, to let the process carry us and shape us, even if we don't want to go and have no idea where the flow is taking us? Do we trust that this process, this flow, is in fact God's river of grace?

Imagine being pressured by your friends to go down the most intimidating waterslide at the amusement park; you are sorry the minute that rushing current carries you away. "Too fast!" you scream as you are swept through a multitude of twists, turns, and tunnels so dark that you can't see your hand in front of your face. You have no idea whether or not you will come out in one piece. At times you cover your eyes because you don't want to see what's coming next. Finally after what seems like an eternity you land with a splash safely in a shallow pool where you catch your breath. Your heart is racing. You may even be angry at your friends for making you go through with it. There's no way you would ever go down that slide again, and yet, at the end, there's this tingling sensation you can't explain, and you wonder: perhaps something *good* came out of that wild ride.

Certainly no one wants to invite illness, death, and grief into their lives, just as no one chooses to suffer. It's hard to imagine that anything good could come out of it, and often we don't find out for a long time just what good was wrought. Yet we know of inspirational stories of people who have gone through tremendous suffering and loss and have come out changed for the better; they even express gratitude over the change despite the difficulties they experienced. They would never have *chosen* to go through their loss, but they *allowed* the grief journey to change them. They were willing to embrace the work involved with grief to see it through, believing that good would come out of it.

Louisa May Alcott wrote in her journal that she was changed for the better by the lengthy illness and death of her younger sister Elizabeth. "Lizzie," like Beth, was a reserved, unassuming young woman who wanted nothing more than to stay close to home and care for her parents. She "spoke" through her many deeds; her sweetness and self-sacrificing love endeared her to many. Opposites in temperament, Louisa and Lizzie enjoyed a close sisterly relationship, taking lessons from the other's strengths. Louisa devoted herself to her sister's care, using her considerable talents as a storyteller and comedic actress to support Lizzie through the long and painful nights. Inspired by her sister's patience through her two years of suffering, Louisa described it in a poem:

> O my sister, passing from me
>   Out of human care and strife,
> Leave me as a gift those virtues
>   Which have beautified your life.
> Dear, bequeath me that great patience
>   Which has power to sustain
> A cheerful, uncomplaining spirit
>   In its prison-house of pain.
>
> Give me—for I need it sorely—
>   Of that courage, wise and sweet,
> Which has made the path of duty
>   Green beneath your willing feet,
> Give me that unselfish nature
>   That with charity divine
> Can pardon wrong for love's dear sake,—
>   Meet heart, forgive me mine![1]

She recalled her sister's willingness to remain engaged with her family and friends even as she prepared to die, as recounted in *Little Women*: "Beth, tranquil and busy as ever, for nothing could change the sweet, unselfish nature, and even while preparing to leave life, she tried to make it happier for those who should remain behind. The feeble fingers were never idle, and one of her pleasures was to make little things for the school children daily passing to and fro."[2]

Lizzie's death signaled a profound change in the tight-knit Alcott family dynamic that had been Louisa's foundation. In her midtwenties, mired in sadness, her family dispersing and no prospects for work or marriage to support her poverty-stricken parents, Louisa nearly took her own life. Inspired by remembrances of her sister and a determination to take care of her family, Louisa mustered her courage, allowing herself to be transformed. It began with the bold move of applying as a Civil War nurse just as women were being accepted into the field; she was hired in part because she had nursed Lizzie. Her experience caring for the many wounded after the brutal Battle of Fredericksburg produced *Hospital Sketches*, her first success as an author. More success would follow as the life-changing power of her struggles (which now included haunting memories of the soldiers she had nursed, plus her own long recovery from typhoid pneumonia) continued to infuse her work with heart, truth, and real life as never before. It would enable her to pen the classic book that would resonate with countless girls from around the world for nearly one hundred and fifty years. As a result she was able to finally relieve the chronic poverty of her family, allowing her to keep her promise to her beloved mother made long ago in childhood:

> I hope that soon, dear mother,
> You and I may be

In the quiet room my fancy
Has so often made for thee,—

The desk beside the window
Where the sun shines warm and bright
And there in ease and quiet
The promised book you write,

While I sit close beside you,
Content at last to see
That you can rest, dear mother,
And I can cherish thee[3]

I believe that caring for and losing her sister acted as a
catalyst to Louisa May Alcott's transformation as an artist and a
woman. The creative gifts of storytelling, play acting, and humor
that she had used to minister to Lizzie were subsequently shared
with countless soldiers, helping them to while away their lonely
hours of pain. Letters sent home to family told the stories of
the wounded. These stories, laced with humor and told with
urgent realism and heart, compiled *Hospital Sketches*, a book
that resonated with thousands of readers anxious for those first-
hand accounts. Louisa's creative gifts were honed and perfected
through her painful journey.

This nineteenth-century author now was helping me to
understand my own grief. She, like me, seemed to find an energy
in grief and took action to work through it. We shared a common spirituality even though our religious backgrounds were
quite different (I being Catholic, she influenced by her father's
Transcendentalism). To her, God was a loving Father and faithful Friend who revealed himself in nature and in everyday life.
I too related to God in this fashion, seeing him in the natural
world and in people around me, feeling him through the love
of family and friends, tasting and being nourished by him in the

sacred bread and wine, and discerning him through prayer, the scriptures, and reflection.

Her description of consolation in the face of grief through the character of Christie Devon in *Work: A Story of Experience* struck a chord; Christie had recently lost her husband David in the Civil War. I wrote the following on my blog:

> Sitting in David's room one day, surrounded by his things, Christie experiences the sign she sought. . . . She can "hear" the music of that flute that she once dubbed as David's "voice," expressing all the joys and sorrows of his life that he never shared in words. The sign had been given:
>
> "Ah, yes! this was a better answer than any supernatural voice could have given her; a more helpful sign than any phantom face or hand; . . . for it brought back the memory of the living, loving man so vividly, so tenderly, that Christie felt as if the barrier was down."[4]

This was my experience through the many signs with which God graced me as I mourned over my parents. Time and again I encountered what Louisa described so beautifully, and because of that, I simply could not feel sad. When doubts arose as to whether my prayers had been answered, I turned to the scriptures to read again of the thief on the cross, shown mercy by Jesus simply for asking to be remembered.

This new tributary I was exploring began to change me. My understanding of what I read deepened. Reading broadened my thinking and sharpened my mind. I developed compassion for people I previously had judged. I embraced the gray areas of life when before I had shied away from them; I came to enjoy pondering the mysteries of life and of God. The scriptures became alive for the first time; often I sensed God "chattering" at me as my mind and heart were bombarded with insights. Prayer at times moved beyond words to contemplation. My capacity to receive grace expanded as the river poured into me. All during this time I was bringing Communion each week to Jackie. Could being so close to the Eucharist on such a regular basis and sharing it with someone I loved be fueling that grace?

Anatole Broyard, former writer, critic, and editor of the *New York Times,* wrote an essay describing how reading helped him through his terminal cancer. To one author he wrote, "Art is our ace in the hole. I'm eating your book for lunch, and it's making me hungry."[5] This is exactly how I felt whenever I read a book; I felt full and hungry at the same time. St. Thérèse of Lisieux shared in *Story of a Soul* about her love of reading, claiming she would have spent her life at it had she not entered Carmel. Seeking to nourish her heart and mind with insight about her life and faith, she had an insatiable appetite.[6] So did I. As I continued to feed my head, my soul also was being fed. I imagined my mother as my muse, enjoying spirited conversations with me as I shared what I was learning. I longed for her to be here in person to experience my exhilaration.

Ezekiel 36:26 summed up what was happening: "A new heart I will give you, and a new spirit I will put within you." St. Paul reinforced what I was feeling: "Everything old has passed away; see, everything has become new! All this is from God" (2 Cor 5:17–18). God was doing something new with me, but as yet, I had no sense of where to go with it except just to let it happen. I felt like a caterpillar in a cocoon: loved, cared for, filled with good things that assuaged my grief and drew me out of my numbness. Joyce Rupp writes that we need to "give ourselves to the human journey and try not to by-pass it because it is in and through our humanness that we discover the beauty of the inner terrain. It is through this that we are transformed into who we are meant to be."[7]

It's not easy to allow yourself to be transformed. I think of that scripture passage where Jesus describes cloth and wineskins: "No one sews a piece of unshrunk cloth on an old cloak, for the patch pulls away from the cloak, and a worse tear is made. Neither is new wine put into old wineskins; otherwise, the skins burst, and the wine is spilled, and the skins are destroyed; but new wine is put into fresh wineskins, and so both are preserved" (Mt 9:16–17).

I always had a hard time interpreting this passage since I have no direct experience with or knowledge of wineskins. As well, most garments don't shrink today. However, a little research revealed that wineskins were made out of the skin of goats. At first the skin would be flexible and thus able to contain the wine, which continued to ferment, stretching the skin. Eventually, however, the skin would dry up and no longer be flexible. If new wine was poured in, it would burst the skin wide open.[8]

Occasionally we still encounter fabrics that shrink. How many of us have had that unpleasant experience of throwing a favorite garment in the dryer only to have it come out two sizes smaller? Therefore we can imagine what would happen if we tried patching something without first testing the fabric.

I began to see wineskins and garments as metaphors for my inner self and my ability to change. How rigid was I in my beliefs? Was I mired in old ways, unable to bend?

Flow Lesson 9

Bending and Breaking

Materials needed: bible, pen or pencil and paper, uncooked spaghetti, one balloon (not inflated), water

Before beginning this exercise, take a few moments to be still and sense the presence of God within you. Ask the Holy Spirit to guide you through this activity and reveal what he wants you to know.

Read Matthew 9:16–17: "No one sews a piece of unshrunk cloth on an old cloak, for the patch pulls away from the cloak, and a worse tear is made. Neither is new wine put into old wineskins; otherwise, the skins burst, and the wine is spilled, and the skins are destroyed; but new wine is put into fresh wineskins, and so both are preserved."

Write down any impressions you have of these verses: Is the meaning clear to you? How do these verses apply to your life? If the meaning is not clear, ask the Holy Spirit to reveal to you some insight; do not be concerned if the answer does not come right away.

Keeping those verses in mind, take several pieces of uncooked piece of spaghetti and examine them carefully; write down a short description of the strands, including their texture and shape. Now slowly break them in half, making note of any details in the breaking. Note *how* you break them. Describe any sounds you hear as they break. Write down any words that come to mind as a result of the uncooked strands and breaking.

Cook the strands you just broke. Take the cooked strands and repeat the process, first examining them and then breaking them, noting in particular how you break it and whether or not it is easier or harder to break than when they were uncooked. Consider using a knife or scissors to cut them if you cannot break them. Write a brief description of what happened when you broke the spaghetti strands:

- How did they differ?
- Which broke more easily?

- Which spaghetti strands best describe your reaction to change in your life?

- Consider the process that made the cooked strands more pliable, how water and heat (i.e., fire) were involved in that process. Do you see a connection between these two elements and God's Holy Spirit? Describe your impressions.

Another way to illustrate this verse involves a balloon, imagining it as a new wineskin. Write down a short description of the balloon before doing anything with it. What does it look like? How does it feel?

Now fill the balloon with water as if you were filling a wineskin with new wine. Describe the look and feel of the balloon filled with water. Notice the difference in weight between the unfilled and filled balloon. What time of your life is best represented by the empty balloon? What time is represented by the full balloon? Write down your impressions and feelings.

Go back now to Matthew 9:16–17. Did the exercises with the spaghetti and the balloon help to clarify the meaning of these verses? How? What do these verses mean to you now?

Offer a prayer to God describing your feelings with regard to this exercise and how it applies to your life.

Being Led

Is it more painful to try and hold on to these old ways or to go with the flow and allow change to happen? Truthfully, both ways are difficult, but only one way moves us forward toward something better. The disciples had to experience a great deal of suffering before they came to know where Jesus was leading them. They had to endure his death along with their fear, confusion, loss of faith, and guilt before they came to the glorious knowledge of his resurrection and its implications. When they received the Holy Spirit on Pentecost, their transformation was complete; they were able to proclaim the Good News of Jesus boldly throughout the world. Their ultimate reward was eternal life with their beloved Lord.

One disciple, however, would not follow. Judas, perhaps mired in his old ways, ended up betraying the master whom he had loved. His interior wineskin, once supple, was now dry and inflexible. He could not move forward to embrace all that Jesus was offering him. The result was that, after he betrayed his friend, regret and despair consumed him, causing him to take his own life. I cannot help now but feel compassion for Judas, having both experienced and witnessed that despair on a personal level.

Like the eleven, I was fortunate to be graced with the ability to be flexible, to accept the new wine into my wineskin. Rather than dismiss my interest in Louisa May Alcott and my blog as a frivolous waste of time, I accepted the blessing given to me and I was grateful. Rather than chastise myself because my grief wasn't playing out the way I thought it should, I decided to dig deeper through prayer, reflection, reading, and writing to explore it. Rather than relive my regrets over not offering my mother more consolation, I asked God to forgive me and looked for chances to offer consolation to others (which began with bringing Communion to Jackie). In short, I chose to trust God even if I did not understand where I was being led.

I reflected on the sweet sense of fullness and peace whenever I went out in the kayak, the flow of the river leading me to new vistas to explore. I equated that flow of the river to God's grace and the promise I made to float downstream with him. I am just beginning to integrate this feeling of letting go into every aspect of my life, since there are many parts I still need to release.

By exploring my grief, I realized that the crying part had been delayed. Four years later the tears came. The outbursts are more frequent now, usually prompted by something I have seen; old movies and TV shows make effective catalysts. Sometimes it happens in public, that sudden rush of tears coupled with a painful longing coming up from the gut like vomiting. It overwhelms me for a few moments and then passes quickly like a summer storm. While it is disconcerting for my grief to be displayed in front of others, I recognize it as a normal part of the process.

I am beginning to better relate to the grief of my siblings, which has produced honest sharing, greater closeness, and healing in our relationships. We often reflect on how much we love our parents and what they did for us. In thinking more deeply about my father, I have come to a better understanding of my brother, and as result, we have grown closer. My sister and I often talk at length about how we feel and how grief has changed us. She too has undergone a rebirth of a passion long dormant. In an e-mail to me she wrote, "Perhaps when you have a loss you go back to your roots to help rebuild. My interest in painting came alive again fueled by knowing my parents would be very happy about that. Perhaps their spirits continue to reside within me and urge me on." By talking it out with her, I realized the same thing was happening to me.

Part of the grief process can manifest itself in a fascination with the past. Now that I have inherited many of the old family portraits, photo albums, and papers from my parents, our son and daughter have become interested in family history. A cherished item is a massive collage of pictures my mother put together for my father for their fiftieth wedding anniversary, which features memorable moments in our family; it hangs in our dining room just as it used to in theirs. In talking over the lives, passions, talents, and personality traits of their grandparents, Stephen and Meredith have learned about themselves just as I have; it's a bittersweet form of grieving that we all find very meaningful. I have urged our children to ask us questions, to get to know their mother and father as people, because that longing to know will intensify once we are gone. As I see my parents' legacy coming to life inside of me and my siblings, I am filled with questions; there aren't nearly enough family papers to satisfy my curiosity, and too many people in the old photographs are not identified. Those questions will now have to wait until our reunion in eternity.

Flow Lesson 10

Exploring Your Family Heritage

Materials needed: immediate family members; photo albums, family papers, and letters; a plan to visit the cemetery or town where previous generations lived

This is a wonderful exercise for expanding the understanding of the fourth commandment: "Honor your father and your mother" (Ex 20:12). The Bible is replete with family history, including the lengthy genealogy of Jesus Christ in the first chapter of Mathew's gospel. We continue to honor our parents who have passed on by carrying on certain family traditions and legacies. This can also apply to a beloved aunt, uncle, cousin, child, or friend. As I have discovered the traits I share in common with my parents and grandparents, I am motivated to continue digging deeper into my life to find more. Knowing their history gives new purpose and meaning to what I do.

Take a day to get together with your spouse and children and explore the history of the families of your mother and father. Before beginning this exercise together, take a moment to be quiet and sense the presence of God; recite the Our Father together. Turn to Matthew chapter 1, and look over the many generations leading up to the birth of Christ. Consider how this genealogy was preserved even before the days of printed books, demonstrating the sacred nature of honoring our ancestors.

Look at family photos together; go through old papers, diaries, and letters; and visit the cemetery or the town of your family's origin. You might want to bone up on some history of the town to give some background as to how people lived during the time your parents were young. Encourage your children to ask questions about you by sharing episodes in your life of which they may not be aware.

These questions can act as a guide in connecting your life with that of your ancestors:

1. In comparing yourself to your mother, father, grandmother, or grandfather, what personality traits do you see in any of them that are in you? Are you happy with those traits? If so, how can you honor that person with that trait within you? If you are not happy with that trait, what can you do to turn it from something negative to something positive?

2. What talent, ability, or interest do you share with a parent or grandparent? What can you learn from your parent or grandparent's life that will help you make the most of your gift? How can you honor your parent or grandparent with your use of this gift?

3. Find out more about the religious heritage of your parents and grandparents and how their faith was commonly practiced

in their day. How has that heritage affected your faith? What religious traditions did your parents and grandparents practice that you could continue to practice in your own home?

End the exercise with drawing out a family tree together, seeing how far back you can go. Beyond listing names and dates, see if you can also add a brief description of your ancestors, perhaps even adding a photograph or a sample of their handwriting. You may want to check out ancestry.com to trace your family history.

Comings and Goings

However our grief journey works out, it will ultimately change us. Joyce Rupp writes, "We let go of the way we have known, we lose the way, we search for the way, and we find the way. We continually seek meaning in life and ponder the course of our inner direction. We keep coming upon facets of self-truth in us that we never knew existed. Our goodbyes can compel us to enter into deeper, newer territory if only we will continue, even when the going gets rough or the path seems unsure and we want to give up."[9]

Rupp also writes of the "hello" that comes after the "goodbye." By exploring my tributary, I had indeed said hello to a new passion; that passion was about to reacquaint me with a part of myself that had lain dormant for years—rejected, beaten down, misunderstood for what it was supposed to be. It would also introduce me to a new undertaking.

When we say hello to that newly discovered part of ourselves that emerges during the grief journey, we can tap into an amazing adventure that will fill us with joy and gratitude and leave us breathless. We may scratch our heads sometimes and wonder about our sanity. That "hello" will stretch the inner wineskin to the bursting point; yet the skin will not break but instead will continue to grow as grace keeps it together.

It begins with seeing the journey to its next destination and beyond.

Questions for Reflection

1. What are your "one-liners"? How would you use those phrases to describe your response to your grief journey or time of trial?

2. When you are or were in the middle of grief or suffering, do you react as you expect you would? Do you feel compelled to act or do you prefer to withdraw? What does your reaction to suffering tell you about yourself?

3. Louisa May Alcott expressed her grief over the loss of her younger sister in part through her writing and by volunteering as a Civil War nurse. Has your grief inspired some kind of creative response or caused you to make some dramatic change in your life? What was that creative response or change and how has it affected you? How did this change occur? Did it happen quickly or evolve over time?

4. How has the loss of a loved one in your family changed your family dynamic? Is there a relationship that has changed (either growing closer or farther apart) as a result of a death in the family? If family members have drifted farther apart, what steps can you take to try and draw those family members back in?

5. How have grief and trials affected your faith life? In what ways has your faith either grown deeper or lessened? If you find it difficult to attend church or to think about God because of your pain and yet still want to return, what action can you take to begin this journey back? Is there a friend, family member, or church member whom you can call upon to help?

6. Do you feel that suffering is inevitable in order for you to grow as a person? How does that make you feel? How can suffering help you to grow and change? If you feel your life has been transformed in some way, can you trace its beginning back to something specific? What event began the process? How did this event change you?

7. If you have lost your parents, are you now curious as to what they were like as people, beyond their being "Mom" and "Dad"? Have you developed an interest in tracing your family history? How do you encourage your children to ask you questions about who you are? What family stories can you share with them to enlighten their understanding? How have you acted upon discovering more about your family heritage, and what have you learned about yourself as a result?

Visit beasone.org, click on the "Resources" tab and then "Flow Lessons" for additional activities to facilitate a deeper exploration of the concepts of this chapter. Videos, music, and examples are supplied to help you with these exercises.

Chapter 5—Diving Deep

How Daring to Write Released My Creativity

Part of the fun of kayaking on hot summer days is finding a private spot where you can swim. Running my hands through the water or dipping my toes as we paddle along is pleasurable, but not enough when the summer sun bears down. Swimming becomes the goal—a total immersion into the water. That cooling sensation, especially after diving under, brings quick relief from the heat.

I particularly enjoy kayaking and swimming at Walden Pond in Concord. Along with the pristine beauty is its historical significance: Henry David Thoreau had built his one-room cabin near the shore, and the Alcotts were frequent visitors. The clarity of the water is legendary; when conditions are calm and the water smooth as glass, you can see far down to the rocky bottom. Walden may be a small pond, but it is quite deep. There comes a point when you cannot view the bottom. The only way to see beneath the blackness is to take a deep dive below the surface.

The river of grace that exists in each of us beckons us to dive deep, to enter the unknown and discover what lies within. This is signified by our Baptism, when we are either sprinkled or immersed in holy water. Jesus was immersed in the waters of baptism before beginning his public life. Matthew recounts how "when Jesus had been baptized, just as he came up from the water, suddenly the heavens were opened to him and he saw the Spirit of God descending like a dove and alighting on him" (Mt 3:16). In Baptism, we die to our old selves and rise anew, becoming part of the Body of Christ.

That new self lies deep within us, waiting to be discovered. As we were immersed in the waters of Baptism, now we are invited to dive into the river of grace and discover that authentic self within us. We will never find it if we merely remain on the surface. When we take a moment to be still, can we hear the invitation to throw caution to the wind and take the dive? Diving has its risks, but it also promises great adventure. What will we find? Will we like what we find? What will happen to us as a result of our discoveries? *Must* we take that dive?

I had begun to feel that urge. My passion for Louisa May Alcott, the balm to my grief, was growing beyond reading and blogging for my own enjoyment. A large part of me, long forgotten, was stirring inside, coming to life after a long slumber.

Plumbing the depths is not easy. There are times when a bright spotlight is shown on the soul, and we can't bear what we see. Other times we are groping in the dark with no clue as to where we are going; we are only aware of being led. It begins with a longing and with confusion—with numerous little invitations to step out in the world so that we can also step down further within. It requires reflection and action. It also reveals our fears and the need to deal with them. That invitation to go deeper is the call of grace. When we obey that call, we agree to let God be our guide.

I was aware of the paralyzing effect of fear on my life. I did everything I could to avoid offending people, afraid that they would speak ill of me. I would not stand up for myself for fear of not being taken seriously. I balked at any physical risk. Although open and trusting as a child, I became secretive as an adult because I feared being mocked or rejected. I avoided controversy and public displays of my faith. Faintheartedness had certainly manifested itself during my recent losses. My fear had brought me shame and mired me in the mud. It robbed me of the ability to dream.

Now I was being enticed into the unknown; I was being asked to step beyond my limited world, gain a wider vision, and learn how to dream. With clear intent I sought God's guidance in identifying and conquering my fears. The answers did not come all at once but as a series of gentle invitations, easing me into the flow of grace. As a result I was being asked to do things I never would have considered doing in the past.

Remember swimming lessons as a kid? You're afraid to swim in the deep end, and you don't want to try diving. You hem and haw until the instructor gains your trust. I feared trying these things, but my instructor wore me down; I finally swam in the deep end and even jumped off the high diving board! I felt gleeful at my accomplishment.

So it was with this dive. With each yes I gained confidence and felt increasingly empowered. I was doing what seemed foolish, even impossible—and it was exhilarating.

Daring the Next Step

Writing had prompted the urge to dive; the first step was to seek out instruction. Through my blog I became friendly with a published author who taught writing, and she offered to tutor me online. Her instruction and encouragement built my confidence such that I was able to write a short story and a long essay. A dream began to percolate: Could I tackle writing a book?

The groundwork had already been laid due to the demands of my blog. I wanted to expand my research beyond Louisa's stories and biographies of her life in order to continue offering worthwhile content. I had visited the Special Collections room of the Concord Library where I was able to touch pages Louisa had written for *Little Women*, and it whet my appetite for more. The bulk of the family papers are housed at the Houghton Library at Harvard University, so I decided to venture over. Taking that step was huge; I was no scholar and felt out of place on the campus of Harvard. The payoff more than made up for my discomfort. Drawn to Louisa's sister Lizzie, I buried myself in the volumes of family letters and journals to learn more about her. I ended up with pages and pages of notes, enough for a book. There had never been a serious study done on this nearly invisible Alcott sister, and I felt she was misrepresented and misunderstood. Having read Lizzie's own words, I developed a strong connection with her and made it my mission to give her the voice she never had.

This was certainly the craziest invitation yet. How could I, with so little writing experience and no formal education beyond my college degree write such a book? I had no idea how to do it. Saying yes to that call required a lot of trust, but I knew better than to say no.

It was at this point that I received the next invitation: to claim ownership of my writing vocation by vocalizing my intention. A fellow blogger suggested the idea. Jeff Goins, a blogger-turned-author, used his blog to help aspiring writers. He had written a book called *You Are a Writer*, challenging his readers to claim their calling just as he had done. I read the book, took a deep breath one day, and said out loud, "I am a writer." It was a surprisingly hard thing to do, but that declaration set me on the path I knew God wanted me to take.

In the gospels I saw how Jesus encouraged people to voice their intent. He asked the blind man Bartimaeus, "What do you want me to do for you?" and Bartimaeus named his desire: "My teacher, let me see again" (Mk 10:51). He committed to his request by declaring it, and Jesus healed him.[1] Zacchaeus, a chief tax collector despised by the people, was so determined to see Jesus that he risked the mocking of the crowd to climb a tree.[2] He caught the attention of Jesus, who called out to him, asking to come to the man's home. Zacchaeus immediately climbed down and declared his intention to give half of what he owned to the poor and to make restitution. By declaring his intent, Zacchaeus expressed his desire to follow Jesus; the Lord responded, "Today salvation has come to this house" (Lk 19:9).

In order to commit to the deeper life to which God was calling me, I too had to declare my intention. Yet even as I claimed my vocation and applied a more serious application to my writing, I sensed there was more to it. In order to fully embrace it, I had to learn what it truly meant to *create* something. My creative self, long dormant, was waking up and demanding my attention. It was at this critical point that I came upon a book that would serve as my guide. In *The Soul Tells a Story*, author Vinita Hampton Wright explores what is known as the *creative process*, using examples from her own life as a writer to guide her readers. She maintains that the process is spiritual: "If I truly open my eyes and express in words what I have seen, then I will have participated in a spiritual act. I receive the vision from beyond myself, and I express it through who I am."[3] In essence she is describing grace—pure gift, something we can ask for but cannot generate on our own.

In reading about Wright's experiences I realized that the creative process consists of several components:

- You are not in control of the creative act but only a participant.

- You are collaborating with something or someone bigger than yourself.

- You have to work hard and dig deep to unearth the excellence.

- You must be open to change, willing to go along for the ride.[4]

All of these actions become possible within the river of grace. Something felt familiar about this process; it was not unlike what I had just been through with my grief.

I had not been in control of my grief but only a participant. Grief proved to be mysterious and unpredictable. At times my heart and mind would tell me I was at peace with my losses, but my body would indicate otherwise; there were unresolved issues within. Normally control over my life was paramount, but this time I acquiesced. I felt so empty and tired by the time my mother died that I was willing to be carried.

I had been collaborating with something or someone bigger than myself. My interest in Louisa May Alcott was rekindled due to a kindness from my husband. Reading and writing literally fell into my lap; I felt they were gifts from God, acting as agents of consolation, growth, and change. I was happy to accept these gifts and see where they would take me.

I had to work hard and dig deep to unearth the excellence. I questioned why my grief played out the way it did and sought help from our parish priest, a grief counselor, and our parish bereavement group. I spent time with God in prayer, searched the scriptures, wrote in my journal about my feelings, and found answers and consolation in my reading and blogging. In its enigmatic way, grief became the path to transformation.

I was open to change and willing to go along for the ride. As I rode through my grief, I sensed a new season in my life opening before me. I wanted to go along for the ride. Something new was being conceived; grief had proven to be a powerful creative force.

When you hear the word "creative," what pops into your mind? An artist painting a masterpiece? A singer penetrating your heart with her velvety voice? A master ballerina leaving you breathless as you watch her leap to great heights? A writer hunkered down in a cabin in the woods writing the book that would tell the story of your life? Creativity is usually associated with the fine arts, but it applies to so much more.

What about the entrepreneur opening up a hardware store in your town? Or the mother preparing dinner for her family, opting to cook from scratch rather than using pre-prepared, processed food? What about the manager of a company, brain-storming with colleagues on how to market their latest product? Or a committee of women planning a conference that will serve hundreds of participants? In each case something *new* is being generated, with *intent*, working with elements that already exist.

Vinita Hampton Wright writes, "Every human being is creative. When you take the stuff of life and rearrange it so that it matters, so that it does good things, you're acting creatively. You don't have to come up with a new idea to be creative. All you have to do is find an old idea and apply it to a new moment or group of people or situation."[5]

What about you? Is there something you do that creates something new? Even the smallest act has the potential to be creative so long as that act is approached with intent. Something as mundane as changing the sheets on a bed can constitute a creative act. Think for a moment about *why* you do this: Isn't it to *create* a comfortable, clean space? How much care do you put into smoothing out the sheets? Perhaps your mother taught you how to make hospital corners. Doesn't the bed feel and smell fresh, making it inviting to sleep in? I remember my mother faithfully changing the sheets once a week on our beds. I loved turning back the covers and climbing in between the cool, crisp sheets. It was a tangible reminder of my mother's love for me.

I know a priest who celebrates the Mass as an art form. What makes it art is his attention to the ritual. This attention transcends perfectionism; his thorough knowledge of each detail manifests itself in passionate love and reverence for the Mass. I attended one Sunday when I found myself in need of emotional healing. Halfway through, I witnessed Fr. Steven break the large wafer slowly and deliberately into several pieces; he then dropped a small piece into the cup of wine as the choir intoned "Lamb of God, you take away the sins of the world; have mercy on us." I had seen this ritual performed countless times, and yet I felt as if I was seeing it for the very first time. I could hear the soft "crack" as the wafer was being broken, and I thought of Christ, his body broken with open wounds. Watching the piece fall as if in slow motion into the cup, I envisioned the all-too human, bloodied body of Christ. Jesus, fully God and fully human, dying on the cross, utterly alone in his pain yet steadfast in his resolve. Dying for humanity, for me, out of pure love. I wept. Later on when I received, I wept again. Those tears provided healing that day.

Fr. Steven had become an agent of healing grace for me that day because of the way he had celebrated the Mass. His approach illustrates the creative process; he is a full participant in something far greater than himself, having done the digging necessary to achieve excellence through study, practice, and spiritual contemplation. The fruit of his work is seen in the many people who are blessed by the liturgies at his parish. They may not understand why they are attracted; they just know that the attraction is strong. His parish is not my home parish, but it seems that whenever I am in need of healing, I go there. It was at this church that my throat was blessed and my voice restored.

Fr. Steven demonstrated that talent in the fine arts is not necessary for creativity because the process is not based on talent but on a state of perpetual being. Jesus was the perfect example. He recognized that he was merely a participant in his Father's plan ("I can do nothing on my own . . . because I seek to do not my own will but the will of him who sent me" [Jn 5:30]). Before his entry into public life, he took time alone in the desert to search himself through prayer and fasting, confronting his temptations and fears. Emerging from the desert, he was baptized by John, thus making public the start of his mission. Having plumbed the depths, Jesus was free of uncertainty, bold in his calling yet open and vulnerable to others. He was in perfect communion with his Father, willing at all times to be led, even to the point of his death.

A careful reading of the gospels shows how he lived every moment with intent. He was fully present to anyone who desired to see him, even in the midst of swarming crowds, most especially those in need of healing. He confronted the religious leaders, hoping to shake them out of complacency. He taught the disciples with great patience in an effort to prepare them for what was to come. He poured out his heart to them fully aware that they would desert him, yet also knowing most would return. Despite exhaustion, he prayed into the wee hours of the morning, mindful that this time with his Father would renew his strength.

I began to see that it wasn't just my abilities as a writer or musician that made me a creative person but rather how I lived my life. This deep dive that the Lord was inviting me to take would affect not only my art but *everything* I did. It would change the way I saw the world. It would stretch my mind and heart, revealing a horizon wider than I ever could imagine. It would affect reconciliation within; I would learn to value myself as a child of God and embrace the life he had given to me. By loving myself in this manner, I would learn to love others. *This* is how I would learn to create.

When Jesus admonishes us to be "perfect, therefore, as your heavenly Father is perfect," he means in part for us to become our authentic selves, the people we were created to be (Mt 5:48). When he asks us to follow him, he means that we too must live with intent and be fully present to each and every moment. He is calling us out of the shadows to become whole through his grace. We are *all* called to this creative process because that process is woven in with the spiritual life; it is the driver of spiritual awakening. While we may not be artists, we are people who *create life* for others. Parents make a home for their children, creating a safe haven where each child will be nurtured into healthy adulthood. Business owners create products that serve the public and generate jobs. By running a bake sale, a church group raises funds so that young people can travel to Appalachia and repair the homes of the poor. A man and a woman marry, and by the grace of God, they create a new life through their love.

It is up to us to accept God's invitation and dive deep within ourselves to find out who we are, what we are supposed to create, and to whom we are to give what we have created.

Flow Lesson 11

"Artists" in Our Lives

Materials needed: pen or pencil and paper, bible, music to listen to or an image or candle to gaze upon, note paper, envelopes

Begin by becoming still to sense God's presence. After a few moments, read Psalm 139. After the reading, take a moment to thank God for how special you are in his eyes.

Next, ask God to reveal to you the names of the "artists" in your life: people you know who live with purpose, intent, enthusiasm, and commitment. These are people who create something beautiful and new without necessarily being talented in any of the fine arts. You may want to listen to quiet classical or spiritual music or gaze upon an image of Jesus or a lighted candle as you carefully review all the people in your life.

Once you have compiled a list (and don't be concerned if you can only think of one or two people), take a piece of paper and write the first person's name at the top of the page. List words and phrases that describe what this person creates (for example, my grandmother kept a picture-perfect vegetable garden and used the vegetables to cook sauces; my father built me a dollhouse when I was little, and so on). Start a page for each person that was revealed to you during your prayer time.

Once you have completed your pages, go back and write something about how each person has influenced or inspired you. What was it about what he or she created that made it so memorable and dear to you? Take a moment to thank God for each person and what he or she gave to you. Then, handwrite and address a note to each person, thanking them for what they do and who they are. If a person is no longer alive, keep the note as a memento of that person or send it to that person's children.

Now, take a clean sheet and put your name at the top. Can you think of anything you have created that has impacted someone? What did you create and what was its impact? Do not be concerned if you cannot think of anything creative that you have done—there will be other exercises in this chapter that will help you to discover your special creative gifts.

End your prayer by taking a note card and writing it to God, thanking him for creating you and making you his special child.

Going Deeper

How can we begin to go deeper? If we sense some part of us waking up inside, how do we find out what it is and what we are supposed to do with it? I offer to you a short chronicle of my deep dive as an example of what you can do to start yours. You will see that it can be meandering and at times confusing, painful, and exciting. When diving into the river of grace, you will be reunited with someone long forgotten and meet a part of yourself you have never seen before. I invite you to immerse yourself and allow God to reveal his plans, his aspirations, and his unconditional love.

A deep dive can begin by recalling what we loved to do when we were children, long before adults told us what we should be doing.[6] Perhaps, as my sister had done with her painting, I could go back to my roots as well. By tracing my history maybe I could find a common thread.

I revived an old habit of journaling, which did indeed reveal that common thread. It began in childhood, when an early love of reading spawned two passions. Three books foreshadowed the work that would later consume my life and fill it with such joy.

My favorite was a biography on Louisa May Alcott. Here I was introduced to the woman with whom I so identified. I loved my second favorite book, *Black Beauty*, so much that I wrote a sequel to it and bound it into a book. Other books followed, some coming from ghost stories I told at Girl Scouts camp. Writing manifested itself in plays I wrote and performed with the kids in the neighborhood. Throughout my teenage years I kept a journal.

A third favorite book, *The Secret Raft* by Hazel Krantz, foretold my passion for research, analysis, and insight, which surfaced only in the last few years. In the story, Howie, a twelve-year-old boy who was very smart but bored with school, had been assigned a ten-page paper due in one week for failing to do his social-studies report. At first Howie was overwhelmed by the assignment, but as he began to fill up the note cards with his research, he became lost in the subject. He ended up writing a twenty-page paper. As a kid I remember feeling his enthusiasm and urgency, the pen not moving fast enough to capture the ideas bursting in his head. I was fascinated with how he wrote that paper; little did I know how this story would portend the passion for research I would come to know so many years later.

Reading and writing were not my only interests; music, too, was a staple. Blessed (or cursed) with a loud voice, I loved leading the sing-alongs on the bus to and from Girl Scouts camp. I sang myself to sleep at night. At age fifteen I fell head over heels in love with the guitar. Soon after, I began writing songs fashioned after my muse, Joni Mitchell, whose lyrics inspired a love for words. I experienced success in music, and thus my confidence grew. Writing, on the other hand, was not enjoying such success, so I abandoned it. Or so I thought. In tracing back my history, I realized for the first time that writing had never been abandoned but rather channeled through music.

Think for a moment about the various interests in your life. Were they encouraged? Perhaps they were frowned upon by your parents or teachers. Did you give up on them because you became discouraged? Maybe a pastime you thought long dead actually survived in another form just as my writing endured through songwriting. Could God be inviting you to take another look at that long-dormant interest, just as my sister had done with her painting? Perhaps that interest is the way God intends for you to rebuild your life after the loss of your loved one. Tracing my history was revealing that to me.

Flow Lesson 12

In the Beginning . . . Part One

Materials needed: pen or pencil and paper; favorite childhood books, videos, and songs

Before starting this exercise, take a few moments to be still and sense the presence of God within you. Ask the Holy Spirit to guide you through this activity and reveal what he wants you to know.

Now think back to your childhood and recall your favorite books. Make a list of those books and find copies of them from the library to reread. Now journal about the following questions:

- Did you experience a wave of nostalgia? How did that feel?

- List specific elements of the books that sparked your imagination.

- Has anything from those books figured into your adult life? Why and how? If not, why not? Did you simply grow up and away from the idea, or was the concept suppressed for some reason in your life, either by you or someone else? Would you like to resurrect that idea for your life? Why or why not?

- What do these memories say about you as a person? How is God speaking to you through these memories?

Is there a favorite childhood movie or song that sparks the same reaction? Watch that movie or listen to that song and journal about the above questions.

Channeling Creativity

As an adult I discovered the ugly underbelly of my creativity. In the early part of my married life, I was consumed with music to the exclusion of all else; it was a miracle our relationship survived that period. During that time I was reading a biography on Louisa, which revealed her volatile artistic temperament; it helped me to understand the dizzying highs and lows I was experiencing as an artist. I dubbed this dark side of creativity the "beast." It controlled my emotions and consumed me in self-absorption, turning me into someone I didn't want to be and that no one wanted to be with. My faith life was practically nonexistent during this period, which left me on my own to deal with this "beast." Fearful of its raw power, I put it away, inadvertently suppressing a large part of my creative energy. Only now as I was coming to terms with this part of me did I realize that God could manage the beast and make it work for me.

Motherhood began to free me from self-absorption. I gave up music when I had children, fully aware of the all-consuming nature of both entities. By nurturing the creative lives of my children, I was keeping mine alive as well, although I didn't know it at the time. My son, daughter, and I enjoyed reading together, making up stories and finger characters, playing games, cooking, coloring, painting, and creating art on the computer. I remember my son jumping up and down on our bed while narrating a story, which I quickly captured on the computer; it was as exhilarating as if I had written the story myself. I compiled a notebook of stories and art that my children created; it is now a treasured keepsake for our family.

These memories demonstrated that God had been protecting my creative life all along, despite the fact I hadn't placed it under his control until very recently. I could not hide away his gift; he meant for me to use it. You too could have a gift that you thought was long gone; did God tuck it away in a safe place inside of you until you were ready to use it again? Vinita Hampton Wright explains, "Creative gifts are resilient and quite patient. They appear when the time is right and can adapt to an ever-changing environment. Even after being undiscovered or neglected for decades, they can walk onstage in brilliant clothes and dazzle you and those who are your witnesses."[7] Could your gift have been funneled into another arena such that you might not recognize it? So far I had seen my writing channeled first into music and then into my children as I stimulated their creativity.

Flow Lesson 13

In the Beginning . . . Part Two

Materials needed: pen or pencil and paper, whatever materials you need to relive your favorite childhood activity

Before beginning this exercise, take a few moments to be still and sense the presence of God with you. Ask the Holy Spirit to guide you through this activity and reveal what he wants you to know.

Now recall a favorite creative childhood activity: coloring, playing with dolls or toy soldiers, making houses out of shoe boxes, molding mud pies or playing with clay or Play-Doh, building with blocks or Legos or an Erector set, playing a toy musical instrument, sewing clothes for your dolls, building a race car out of wood, performing science experiments, building electronic gadgets, and so on. Perhaps you put on plays with your friends, ran carnivals to raise money for charitable causes, or created costumes or a haunted house for Halloween. Maybe you collected stamps or a certain toy (I used to collect toy horses); maybe you admired a particular movie or TV star and put together a scrapbook. Go back and revisit your favorite childhood activity and actually engage in that activity again if you can. Stay with it for a while even if it feels strange to you.

Write down what you were feeling while engaged in that activity:

- How did you feel at first as you engaged in this activity? Weird or foolish? Awkward or embarrassed? Happy, sad, or nostalgic? Describe the activity and your reaction to it: Did you experience a déjà vu moment, a rush of memories? Perhaps the activity left you feeling flat—can you recall why you used to like it? Are there people associated with this activity? Who are they and how do you feel as you remember them?

- Did you forget at first how to do the activity? Were you able to eventually reconnect to it, and if so, how? If you were not able to reconnect, how did that make you feel?

- What connection, if any, do you see between that activity and your life today? If it doesn't figure in, do you want it to, and how would you incorporate it?

- Does this activity reveal something about you that was long forgotten? What does the activity say about you? Did it reacquaint you with something long dormant? Describe that connection.

Enter into prayer with God and ask him to reveal to you the meaning of this favorite activity and how it relates to your present life. What is he trying to teach you about yourself? Do not be concerned if the answer doesn't come right away; take your notes and place them where you can see them each day and offer them up to God as part of your daily prayer, asking for his wisdom and insight. Once something is revealed to you, return to your notes and write down what you learned and then thank God for that insight.

Taking Care of Our Gifts

With creativity and spirituality so closely connected, it was not surprising that a faith revival would reawaken the music I had put away. It began with a song about a dear friend's daughter who was dying of AIDS and had returned to her Catholic faith with a vengeance. She had piercing eyes. Hers was a story I just had to get down into a song. I ended up singing the song during her funeral Mass and then had a professional recording made at the request of her mother; she in turn gave copies to family members and friends.

The floodgates opened and songs poured out of me. I started performing at local churches and recorded tapes to sell. It was the beginning of a long and fruitful music ministry that took me to World Youth Day and put me on Catholic television. I lived the dream of recording a CD with a New York producer.

It became all-consuming just as before, but this time I had a family to consider. I struggled for balance, which often created frustration, and it required resourcefulness and willpower to make it all work. It was not always a comfortable fit, but I am grateful that my family was there to keep my feet firmly planted.

I'd like to think that my dedication to my art while still fulfilling my roles as wife and mother left my children with a good example of the hard work and sacrifice necessary to be all we are meant to be. It was hard at times to justify in my mind the time I took away from my family to write and record songs; at the same time, I felt compelled to take that time. This push and pull can be particularly difficult for women since pursuing one's art is often deemed "selfish." Yet suppressing this urge can also be harmful to you and those around you. My vocation as wife and mother always came first, and in those roles, I was committed to being honest with my family as to who and what I was: devoted to them, dedicated to my art, and quite human. I regularly admitted my faults and failings to them.

There was one failing, however, that I did not acknowledge to myself until after I lost my ability to sing. Although I wrote songs about God and I prayed to God when I sang my songs, I did not offer my music *to* God for him to manage; it remained mine. I could not reach true excellence because I broke a cardinal rule of the creative process: I took charge rather than being a participant. It prevented my music from being a part of something greater than me. It also made the juggling act much harder to bear and execute well. After a time, creativity no longer filled me with wonder and excitement; instead music became a job.

Creativity, like all aspects of our lives, goes through seasons of work and rest. If not properly cared for, our inspiration and energy can burn out and break down, just as our minds and bodies do from overwork. When we feel tired and stressed

from work, we recharge minds and bodies with "downtime"—
recreation and relaxation. When we are hungry, we eat good
food and feel satisfied. We exercise our bodies and are rewarded
with a sense of well-being through the release of endorphins.
Creativity as well needs that kind of care. Wright encourages,
"Feed your soul with all sorts of beauty, wonder and intrigue.
Invite puzzles that challenge you, works of art that stretch you
and events that charge you up. Make such fun and inspiration
a regular practice."[8]

    I became so involved with the work aspect of music that I
failed to take proper care of the creativity; I didn't allow myself
the "luxury" of refreshing my creative juices, whether it was
through reading, listening to various styles of music, collaborating with others, and so on. That, coupled with trying to balance
my family with my art without asking for God's help, caused
my creative self to wither; I developed writer's block and was no
longer able to write songs. When my father died, much of my
passion for music went with him. After my mother passed away
and I lost my voice, my music became dormant.

    Tracing my history was the beginning of my deep dive.
While it unveiled writing as the common thread in my creative
life, it also revealed important spiritual lessons about fear and the
need for humility so that I could cede control of my life over to
God. I became cognizant of the mistakes I had made that had
harmed me as a person. Writing, however, was not just the means
to resurrect and redeem my creative life; it was also the tool God
intended for me to use to discover my whole and true self—the
very person that he meant for me to be.

Flow Lesson 14

Tracing Your Life History of Interests and Passions

Materials needed: pen or pencil and paper, ruler

Before beginning this exercise, take a few moments to be still and sense the presence of God with you. Ask the Holy Spirit to guide you through this activity and reveal what he wants you to know.

In this exercise you will be tracing the history of your interests and passions. Consider the following questions:

- What did you enjoy doing as a child?

- Do some of those loves continue into adulthood? How do they manifest themselves now?

- Are there things you did as a child that were abandoned when you became an adult? Would you be interested in doing those things again?

- How does tracing your history reveal who you are?

- Do you recognize an interest that you thought had died but perhaps instead had been kept alive in some other way?

- Do you sense something in you that was kept for safekeeping to be used at a later time? What is that interest? How has it been manifested in your life?

Offer these questions in prayer to God, asking for his guidance.

Next, on a piece of paper positioned horizontally, take a ruler and draw a straight line across the paper; this will be your timeline. Think back over times in your life that you consider important, even if it is a small thing. Draw a notch on your timeline and attach an age to it—for example, "At age five I loved playing in the rain." Don't analyze or think too hard about this part of the exercise, but rather put down any incidents that pop into your mind. There are no "right" or "wrong" answers. If you need to extend your timeline because you run out of room, simply draw another line underneath and continue the exercise.

Once you have filled your timeline, go back over each incident with the above questions as your guide; write your impressions. Once done, can you see any kind of common thread or narrative to your timeline? If you can, write a short story of your life, citing each incident on your timeline, and see what that story reveals to you.

If you cannot see the narrative, talk to God and offer each incident up to him and ask for the guidance to see the connections between each of those times in your life. Reflect carefully on each incident. If the answer doesn't come right away, put away the exercise and ask God to reveal what he wishes you to know in his good time. Keep the exercise in a place where you can easily find it, and if you feel an urge to look at it again, it is likely God wishes to tell you something. It may be necessary to do this exercise in starts and stops as God reveals things to you.

Living with Purpose

Each of us has a purpose for our lives planted at the core of our being. Some of us find out early in life what we are meant to do; others find out at the other end. Some of us sadly never find out. We are longing after something but can't figure out what it is. We are blocked by the wounds of hurtful experiences in our lives that have never been healed, whether it be misunderstanding, lack of success, rejection, illness, abuse, or simply not being loved.

We suffer from fear, unresolved anger, or sadness due to loss and grief. We were made to be whole and healthy people, but life is hard and often unjust, and it takes its toll. Yet it is never too late to find out who we are. It is never too late to be healed and transformed. If we take the time to be quiet and still, to reflect upon our lives and discover those tools that will help us unearth our true selves, we can find out who God meant for us to be. If we fully immerse ourselves in the river of grace, we can be made into the whole and healthy people God meant for us to be. It is a creative process that takes what is old and makes it new.

As I am nearing my sixtieth year, God is offering me that opportunity. My deep dive was not just about my creative life but about pulling *all* the pieces of my life together. My roles as wife of a deacon, mother to grown children, sister, friend, writer, graphic artist, church member, and volunteer; my love of reading, music, nature, cats, current events, learning, and history; and my life as a woman of faith would all combine into one person made whole—Susan. No longer would I compartmentalize my life, hiding parts away from others for fear of being misunderstood or mocked. I would learn to replace fear with confidence, sure of who I was and what I was supposed to be doing. In gratitude, I embraced this second chance and vowed to act on everything I had learned from past mistakes.

I made sure from the start that my writing habit was fed with good reading. I vowed as well to work at mastering my craft with practice. Between writing in my journal, taking instruction from my author friend, and contributing to my Louisa blog, I was supplied with ample opportunity. To underscore my commitment, I dedicated the best hours of the day to the task. As I grew in skill and confidence, I branched out, contributing to *CatholicMom.com* and our diocesan newspaper. I started a second blog, *Be As One*, so that I could write freely about spiritual matters and other interests near and dear to my heart.

In my daily prayers I offer myself to God and ask for the intercession of St. Teresa of Avila and St. Thérèse of Lisieux, both writers. My top priority is to remember who is in charge. The early successes I began to experience as a writer made that easy, for I knew it could not have happened solely on my own power.

While the outer successes were gratifying, the inner growth from my deep dive was even more so. My child's eye opened to the world around me. Walks and kayak trips became times of wonder as God whispered stories to me through the beauty of his world. I was also gaining insight into family members I had previously misunderstood. I remember one day at my sister-in-law's house after enjoying a magnificent meal. It made me sleepy, so I opted out of the conversation and observed my sister-in-law. As Cynthia talked about the history of her house and showed us old photographs and documents I realized that we shared a similar interest. The conversation turned to her many domestic talents, which include gourmet cooking, knitting, and crocheting. In that moment I had an epiphany. Like Fr. Steven's celebration of the Mass, Cynthia raised domesticity to an art form because it was done with great care out of love. Her carefully prepared meals, the beautiful sweaters, quilts, and scarves she knitted—all were given away freely to family and friends. It was her way of showing affection. I had not understood that before.

In the same way I sought to understand my daughter; we were as opposite as we could be. I had asked God to help me figure out what made her tick; soon after she moved out of the house, I began to see who she really was. I discovered her special brand of clear thinking and found myself drawn to her whenever I felt troubled. Her "straight-from-the-shoulder, right-between-the eyes" advice laced with humor always snapped me out of it.

Like her Aunt Cynthia, Meredith had her own way of showing her love and affection, and I have now come to appreciate that.

My "vision" became more penetrating and my observations more detailed. I could feel my capacity for love and compassion growing while my penchant for judgment was shrinking. The world around me and the people beside me became endless metaphors for spiritual truths.

The blessings that poured into me during my deep dive spilled out onto those around me. Family and friends remarked on the change, noting the infectious joy as I'd share what was happening in my life. That zest for life had been one of my mother's most endearing qualities; now I was expressing it, too.

In working through my deep dive I was living the creative process. I accepted my role as participant, relinquishing my need to control; I was collaborating with Someone far bigger than myself. I took on the challenge of the deep dive into the still, dark waters of grace to discover a reawakened creative self, "beast" and all, and I embraced it. I was willing to go along for the ride no matter where it led. I have learned how to dream for the first time in my life, confident that God means for me to dream.

The creative process is actually another name for a way of life, the spiritual life. Vinita Hampton Wright is correct: creativity and spirituality are meant to work together; in fact, they are one. This means that *anyone* who engages in the spiritual life is subject to the creative process. If you recognize and accept the presence within of God's Spirit, you will live a creative life. Since God is limitless, the possibilities of creativity are limitless, too. You only need to believe it and take your own deep dive to discover the authentic person within, the one created in the image and likeness of God, the person you are *meant to be*. Nothing is too small or too insignificant. Nothing is too foolish or crazy. No effort is wasted. God has placed the capability in every person to be "great," even if that greatness is quiet, unassuming, and shared within a small circle. God's capacity for healing is endless, even if it may not be the healing we initially desired. We are asked to accept losses, whether it be loved ones or parts of ourselves, for this is part and parcel of our humanity. Broken as we are, we can be made new, made whole, though likely we will never be the same again. This healing requires shedding the old to embrace the new, just as in the parable of the wineskins. The gospels are replete with broken lives healed and made whole, from the tax collector to the prostitute, from the demoniac to the outcast, from the thief repentant just before death to Lazarus raised from the dead. Being made whole requires submitting to a process of radical change, of being re-created. By being immersed in the river of grace, we can go on the adventure of a lifetime.

A Word to the Wise

No journey should ever be taken alone. As with all adventures, there is risk. Because of the fine line between a legitimate deep dive and self-indulgence and narcissism, such a journey within should be done under supervision. As someone prone to these faults, I learned that, while I should indeed cling to my Creator who knows me best, I also need to continually seek guidance from spiritually mature people. Solitude and quiet are necessary for self-discovery, but so is active engagement with others. Jesus shows us this balance in ministering to so many during the day and withdrawing in prayer overnight. Too much solitude equals isolation, sending us into that delusional bubble where we lose perspective; you come to believe that you alone can accurately discern what God is saying to you. One of the lessons I learned from my deep dive was this necessity to be with others and resist the temptation toward too much solitude. As someone who enjoys her own company, being with others took intent and effort. I found, however, that engagement with community would periodically prick my delusional bubble (a humbling experience!) because I was being held accountable for my actions.

Grief proved to be a most unlikely friend, one that opened the door to a new life. While I would give anything to have my parents back with me again, my faith tells me that we will be reunited someday. I can't help but think that they have been watching over me, perhaps praying for me. All I know is that I am grateful beyond measure for the grace to be open to new possibilities. The ride has not been easy, but I would do it over again. Psalm 139 states that we are "fearfully and wonderfully made" (Ps139:14). That authentic self, placed deep within at the time of Baptism, can take a lifetime to fully emerge. It is the journey of discovery and growth that makes life sweet, full, and worthwhile. It is the kingdom of God within us, revealing to us just who we were created to be.

It is never too late to begin, to take that deep dive for yourself.

Questions for Reflection

1. Recall the fears you identified in chapter 1. How do these fears hold you back? Are you afraid to dream for fear of being disappointed?

2. Recall Bartimaeus and Zacchaeus declaring their intentions. Has God laid an intention on your heart that you need to declare out loud? What is that intention? Declare it out loud to God. How did you feel after declaring it? What do you think will happen next?

3. Has grief created a new season in your life? How do you feel about where you are now? Are you aware of something inside of you wishing to come to the surface? What are specific and practical steps that you can take to discover that "hidden" you? If you don't know where to begin, what can you do to find out what steps to take?

4. In what ways are you creative? List three things that you do with the intention of creating something new for someone else. How do you create life for others?

5. Do you sense the Lord calling you out of the shadows? Are there parts of your life kept secret from others or even from yourself? Are there unresolved conflicts with which you need to reconcile? How can you begin to bring forth those parts of yourself that you have kept hidden from others and yourself?

6. Have you had to say no to something in order to say yes to something new? Did your response have anything to do with the core interests in your life? Did it feel like an invitation from God? How did you respond?

7. What makes someone a "great" person? Does your definition of greatness differ at all from what the world deems as great? Do you feel you have potential for greatness? Why and how?

Visit beasone.org, click on the "Resources" tab and then "Flow Lessons" for additional activities to facilitate a deeper exploration of the concepts of this chapter. Videos, music, and examples are supplied to help you with these exercises.

Chapter 6—Testing New Waters

Why I Believe Anything Is Possible

I am completely at home in a kayak. A powerboat is a different story. I had a chance once to drive one at my sister's camp. Christine and her husband, Tom, invited us out for a ride, and Tom suggested I try driving the boat. Unfamiliar with powerboats, I wasn't keen on the idea for fear of crashing it. Tom insisted it was easy, so I took the wheel. He instructed me to gun the motor, and immediately the bow of the boat went way up in the air; I couldn't see what was in front of me! Tom encouraged me to keep going at that speed so that the boat could level out. I did, clutching the wheel in fright. After what seemed an eternity, the boat finally leveled out. I drove around the lake but never let up on my iron grip of the wheel; the force of the boat scared me. Shortly thereafter I gave the wheel back to Tom. He congratulated me on giving it a try, and that made me feel good. In time I think I could have learned to enjoy the thrill.

Driving that boat had put me out of my comfort zone, and it was disquieting. How do you feel when you step out of yours? A journey into self-discovery requires not only prayer and reflection but action—you have to be willing to step out. Sometimes it begins with a simple invitation to try something new.

Other times you experience a sudden life change, which requires you to react. You have a choice of complying or resisting what is placed before you. The river of grace is there to supply you with strength and sustenance as you venture forth. In doing so you can experience a myriad of sensations from enticement and excitement to feeling disturbed, grieved, unsettled, or unnerved. If you can remain in the river and persevere through the discomfort, you will emerge changed. Whether or not it is positive depends upon your willingness to embrace what is happening. Whatever change you do experience will affect those around you. Some will delight in the "new" you, while others may disapprove or not understand. A test of the soul can be a risky proposition.

My journey of self-discovery began with the chaos and pain of loss, eventually mitigated by the happenstance of reading and writing. I have discovered my vocation of writing, the first invitation to step out. Self-discovery also revealed the tyrannical grip of fear on my life. In asking God to help me overcome my fears, I opened the door to further chances to step out.

That next opportunity came from my husband. Rich had been a leader on the Confirmation retreats at our parish for many years. He loved the work and wanted me to share in it. I kept turning him down, using the excuse of having to stay home with the kids. My real problem was my fear of teenagers. Even though I had successfully raised two, they were my children, and I knew them well. I didn't know other people's children, and I wasn't sure I could relate to them. If I had known I would be reliving my own painful memories of adolescence, I never would have gone.

Accepting Rich's invitation, I accompanied him on my first Confirmation retreat weekend. Being with the young people triggered some of my deepest fears, which manifested themselves in obsessive–compulsive behavior. Such behavior made me late for activities, and I couldn't stop myself from doing them. The irony played out in a prayer service I conducted for the kids. I asked them to imagine all their concerns about home and school, family and friends, as items on a large table. I demonstrated how, with the wave of an arm, they could sweep everything off of their table. This exercise would leave their minds and hearts clear and open for what would happen on the retreat. I was telling them to try something that I was unwilling to do myself.

What was I so afraid of? Since we had each been given a journal, I decided to write about my fears. I found myself describing the same pain I had journaled about as a teenager. I felt raw and insecure; my skin was crawling. Once again I was the outsider, not part of the "cool" crowd. Like before, I just wanted a trapdoor to open up under my feet so I could drop through and disappear. I felt trapped within myself and wanted to break out.

There was another problem: the long shadow of my husband, who was so at ease on the retreat. He could crack jokes on cue and gave off that "cool" vibe, which drew the kids to him. There was no way to compete; he excelled at everything I longed to be able to do but could not. How could I ever conquer my fear and fit in?

The last talk of the weekend provided the means. Gloria, the youth minister, shared about her time spent in Haiti supporting the work of a priest at an orphanage and hospital. Fr. Rick Frechette had been a friend of hers for years and had issued the invitation to come and see. On her first visit she fell in love with the people and returned subsequent times, even bringing her husband and children with her during Christmas. I listened with my mouth open, amazed at her enthusiasm, confidence, and commitment to her mission. I wondered how she had found the courage to go to Haiti, and I remember saying to myself, "Gloria, I want to go wherever you are going." Little did I know that I had just prayed to God for direction; soon the answer would come.

Gloria sensed my interest in the young people despite my fear and asked if I would be willing to substitute teach one night for a tenth-grade class. I was tempted to say no but then wondered if this, too, was an invitation from God. Determined not to let fear get the better of me, I said yes and taught my first class. Gloria e-mailed me a few days later to say that the students reacted well to my class. More invitations came, and I accepted them. Halfway through the year the big one came: Could I take over a class for the rest of the year for another teacher? I accepted. I muddled through that half year, oftentimes going by sheer instinct. The following year I surprised myself by volunteering to teach Confirmation students.

The beauty of accepting invitations from God is that he always provides, and sometimes with a sense of irony. I found my footing by drawing upon those skills I had acquired in college while getting my teaching degree (a degree I had never before used). It tapped into yet another long-dormant area of my creativity as I drew up lesson plans, created visuals, and made the classroom welcoming. In finding my own style of teaching, I no longer felt uncomfortable *acting* like a teacher.

Rather than just convey facts, I wanted to help my students experience their faith. I loved dreaming up methods for them to learn about different ways to pray, through carefully led meditations using art, music, candles, and scented oils. During a lesson on the Eucharist, I took them over to the church to sit by the tabernacle as I sang to them.

I worked to create a safe haven where doubts and questions could be discussed freely. While I didn't have Rich's knack for generating conversation, there were times when fruitful discussions occurred. As I continued to pray for guidance, I could feel my confidence growing. I took my students into my heart and prayed for them. I began receiving positive feedback from parents.

I had stepped out and succeeded. I fought through my fear and allowed God to teach and lead me. I stopped competing with Rich, trusted my instincts, and found my own ways to connect with the students. By accepting Gloria's invitations and opening myself up to the unknown, I not only learned how to share the faith of the Church with young people; I learned to love them. The gift of grace bestowed powerful weapons in my arsenal to fight fear: a core belief in God's love for me and the benefit of loving others through generous giving.

Flow Lesson 15

Take a Chance!

Materials needed: pen or pencil and paper, computer or tablet

Before beginning this exercise, take a few moments to be still and sense the presence of God within you. Ask the Holy Spirit to guide you through this activity and reveal what he wants you to know.

Watch a video of an extremely scary roller coaster ride. (Visit beasone.org, click on the "Resources" tab and then "Flow Lesson 15" to find the video.)

How did that video make you feel? Would you ever go on a ride like that? Why or why not? If you recall going on such a ride, describe the different physical sensations you experienced:

• What was your emotional reaction?

• Is the excitement of a thrill ride fun for you? Why or why not?

- Have you ever ridden a thrill ride feeling utterly terrified at first but then deciding you enjoyed the ride at the end? Can you remember how that made you feel? Did you try the ride again?

Recall a time in your life when you were asked to try something new, something outside of your comfort zone. It can be as simple as going on a thrill ride.

- Did you trust the person or persons who asked you to step out?

- Did you feel pressured to try it? Did you feel supported by the people who asked you to step out, or did you feel as if you were on your own?

- How did you feel toward them after the experience? Write down your impressions.

Consider these verses from Romans 8:26–28: "Likewise the Spirit helps us in our weakness; for we do not know how to pray as we ought, but that very Spirit intercedes with sighs too deep for words. And God, who searches the heart, knows what is the mind of the Spirit, because the Spirit intercedes for the saints according to the will of God. We know that all things work together for good for those who love God, who are called according to his purpose."

Is there a time when you felt a nudge from God to try something new? Describe this experience through these questions:

- Did you trust that God meant for the experience to be for your benefit? What did you experience that made you feel he was with you every step of the way? What did you do to remain in his presence? Do you believe God is with you even if you didn't feel his presence? What can you do to call upon him?

- How did you feel when you first tried the experience?
- How did you feel when the experience was over?
- What did you learn? Did your life change at all from the experience?

Is there a time when you wanted to try something new and different but you lacked the confidence? What is it that you want to try? Listen to the song by Jana Stanfield called "If I Were Brave" and imagine yourself venturing forth, empowered by the Holy Spirit. (Visit beaone.org, click on the "Resources" tab and then "Flow Lesson 15" to find the video.)

Take some time to be quiet with God and share with him how you feel after listening to the song. Read the verses from Romans again, and then picture yourself stepping out and trying the action with Jesus at your side. Write down the action you wish to take, place it somewhere you will see it each day, and offer that action to God in prayer for one week. If you discern that God is inviting you, take steps to set that action in motion. If you are still unsure, talk it over with a friend or your parish priest—it may be that God wishes to reveal his will to you through that person.

Stepping Out in Faith

I saw yet again that working through my fear was necessary in order to find and then *be* my authentic self. I *could* be like Gloria: passionate, confident, joyful, and enthusiastic, affecting those around me as a result. By believing in God's love for me, I could then become his emissary. I didn't have to travel to Haiti; I only had to travel within to discover where the river of grace was leading me, and then commit to the journey. I had to get used to living with the uncertainty that is the fundamental part of self-discovery. It required being alert and awake to that quiet voice of God inside of me, his gentle hand nudging me this way and that. It gave new meaning to Jesus' admonishment to "Beware, keep alert" (Mk 13:33). We must be alert and awake at *all* times to God's call. This is what it means to be truly present to each and every moment. And if we pay heed to such moments, we won't have the time to worry about the future or regret the past.

The changes that happen within you affect those around you. A transformed life can act as a magnet just as Gloria's life attracted me. There are times, however, when a transformed life meets resistance, especially from those we love. How do you deal with the questions and the pushback? What happens if you're not taken seriously? It can be hurtful when those we love do not understand.

Back in 2000, Rich received an invitation that would set him off on a most unexpected journey. Beginning as a simple ripple, it grew over time into a large wave that swept many of us along with him. Some of us emerged pleased with the change, while others were not so sure.

It commenced with a visit to a church. Rich was chaperoning a group of young people from our parish, St. Luke's, on a field trip visiting various Catholic churches in Worcester. Upon entering Our Lady of Perpetual Help Melkite Church, Rich was immediately struck by the interior, which did not resemble a typical Catholic church but was instead filled with beautiful icons. As he listened to the pastor, Fr. Paul, explain the nature of this Eastern Catholic church, Rich felt a deep attraction. The feeling lingered long after the tour was over, and he knew he had to explore the Eastern Church in greater detail.

Rich felt conflicted over his interest in this church; it was calling him to a new and unfamiliar place. He had been very happy with his life at our parish, serving on the parish council, leading the youth choir, teaching high school CCD, and being a retreat leader. Why could he not get this Melkite church out of his mind?

To satisfy his curiosity he turned to the Internet for information; that research led him to key books on the Eastern Church. Each Tuesday evening he visited St. Luke's during adoration to study and reflect. Since the traditions of Melkite Catholics reflected Greek or Byzantine culture and thus closely resembled the Orthodox Church in style and appearance, Rich focused on the works of Kalistos Ware and Theophan the Recluse, both of which provided thoughtful explanations of the Orthodox form of worship. The Melkite Church was clearly Catholic in its allegiance to the pope, but its heart and thinking lay in Eastern ways.

I watched as he devoured book after book. He was excited about his faith on a much deeper level. I began to realize he could end up leaving St. Luke's, and I didn't know how that would affect us as a family. Yet it pleased me to see Rich so passionate about his faith. We had never really shared our personal spirituality with each other before, but now he couldn't stop talking about what he was learning. Every Tuesday he would come home from adoration and read portions of the books he was studying out loud to me. While I didn't understand it all on an intellectual level, in my heart I knew it was good.

We both realized that his exposure to the Eucharistic Lord while reading and studying had to be a key factor in his journey. I am convinced that such close proximity to the living Body and

Blood of Christ week after week enhanced Rich's understanding of his reading, thus making for deep and prayerful reflection. The essence of Christ hidden in the host yet on display during this time of adoration seemed beautifully symbolic to me of Rich's authentic self, hidden within but slowly coming to the surface for all to see.

After several months of study, Rich suggested we attend a Divine Liturgy at Our Lady of Perpetual Help as a family. While the rest of us found the service foreign with its continuous chanting, long prayers, and incense that smelled like bacon, Rich was more attracted than ever. Our children did not get it at all; nor did I. But I knew this church was having a profound impact on Rich's spiritual life, and that's all I needed to support him in his journey.

After two years of study, Rich decided that he would spend the season of Lent at Our Lady of Perpetual Help. I knew this was coming and gave him my blessing. That first Sunday he was "adopted" by a kind woman named Ruth, who carefully explained the basics of worship to him. He met with Fr. Paul on several occasions for spiritual direction to discern whether this attraction to the Melkite Church was for the right reasons. By the time Lent was over, Rich had committed himself to the Eastern Catholic Church. He immersed himself completely in the life of his new parish, eventually becoming an official member.

There were consequences to this decision. With mixed emotions he had to say a final goodbye to St. Luke's, the parish that had been his home for more than twenty years. Leaving behind his work with the young people was especially difficult. It also meant that we would no longer attend church together. Our friends at St. Luke's were confused by Rich's decision to switch parishes; most people knew nothing about this "best kept secret" within the Catholic Church.

Rich's formation, however, was just beginning. Soon he felt the calling to become a deacon in the Melkite Church. This was a decision that would not only change his life but mine as well. While the idea of Rich's becoming a deacon seemed right, I was afraid of what my role would be. I remained Roman Catholic, and yet I was to be the wife of a deacon in the Eastern Catholic Church. How could this possibly work?

Our children were confused and upset by his decision, dismayed at how his new life consumed him. His mother, sister, and brother misunderstood and thought he was leaving the Catholic Church; he had to keep reassuring his family that, yes, he was still Catholic. My family didn't get it either. Rich experienced a variety of reactions ranging from bewilderment and confusion to hostility and alienation.

After much discussion, I agreed to Rich's desire to pursue his calling. We both smiled at the irony of knowing that Fr. Paul was in charge of the deacon program; God has a good sense of humor. While the next four years entailed sacrifice on our part as Rich continued with his studies, I was fortunate to be able to sit in on some of his classes and get to know his classmates. The experience eased me into the Eastern Church, and I enjoyed learning about it. By September 2009, Rich was ordained as a deacon, taking on the name "Elias"; he was assigned to Our Lady of Perpetual Help. While some family members still did not understand, everyone was proud of Rich on his ordination day. I knew it had taken great courage for him to follow through on this most unlikely turn in his life. While I remain Roman Catholic and we belong to different parishes, we are proud to tell everyone of our "East-West" home. Rich's journey brought us closer together as a couple, deepening our love and understanding for each other. This test of his soul changed both of our lives for the better.

By stepping out in faith, Rich stepped down deeper within himself. It propelled him on a very different course without knowledge of where he would end up. It meant dealing with negative reactions and misunderstanding from those closest to him. It also meant sacrificing an old life that had been satisfying and meaningful. The disruption, although painful at times, produced the desired result: the creation of a new season in his life, one rich in spiritual growth that produced deep joy and gratitude. Rich had gone through a creative process of spiritual growth, stretching his mind and heart to the limit, testing his courage, and eventually creating that new life.

Flow Lesson 16

Lost and Found

Materials needed: pen or pencil and paper, computer or tablet

Before beginning this exercise, take a few moments to be still and sense the presence of God within you. Ask the Holy Spirit to guide you through this activity and reveal what he wants you to know.

Recall a time in your childhood when you got lost. Perhaps it was at the supermarket when you couldn't find your mother. Perhaps it was out in the woods. Write down how you felt:

- Were you afraid? Describe the physical sensations and then describe your feelings.

- How did you feel when your mother or father finally found you?

- Is this an important memory in your life? Why or why not?

Think, too, of a time when you were driving to a new place and you got lost. Perhaps you were driving in the city and your destination was a couple of blocks away, but you were stuck on one-way streets, going around in circles with no way to pull off the road to consult a map or GPS. Perhaps you were in the middle of nowhere. Write down how you felt:

- Did getting lost frustrate, frighten, or even panic you? How or why? Describe your physical as well as your emotional sensations.

- How long did it take before you found your way? How did you feel?

Listen to the song by Jana Stanfield called "I'm Not Lost, I Am Exploring." (Visit beasone.org, click on "Resources" tab and then "Flow Lesson 16" to find this video.) Have you ever felt like this?

Describe a time in your life when you were uncertain about where you were headed:

- Did you feel you were alone or did you feel God was with you? Did you call upon God to be with you? Describe the response you felt from him.

- Do you feel lost in your life or perhaps in a holding pattern at this time? Do you know why you feel lost? Describe your feelings. If you are in limbo, how are you coping with the waiting? What value do you see, if any, in the waiting?

- Does your life feel like an adventure to be experienced, a trial to be endured, or simply a day-to-day occurrence that is unexciting? What steps can you take to effect a change?

At the end of your notes, copy the following prayer by St. Ignatius of Loyola: "Take, Lord, and receive all my liberty, my memory, my understanding, and my entire will, all that I have and possess. Thou hast given all to me. To Thee, O Lord, I return it. All is Thine; dispose of it wholly according to Thy will. Give me Thy love and thy grace, for this is sufficient for me."[1]

Now say the prayer out loud, offering your time of uncertainty and waiting to God. Keep this prayer with you so that you can repeat it each day. After one week, revisit these questions and your notes, and see if your answers have changed.

You can also listen to a musical version of this prayer by the St. Louis Jesuits on YouTube: "Take Lord, Receive" by John Foley, S.J. (Visit beasone.org, click on "Resources" tab and then "Flow Lesson 16" to find this video.)

Necessary Growth

The soul was not meant to be stagnant. We may find ourselves enticed, nudged, pushed, and sometimes even thrown into the river of grace in order to take that deep dive into self-discovery and spiritual growth. It's what we do once we are immersed that determines the outcome. We will experience pain in our growth due to resistance, either because we are afraid or because others push back on us. God's grace provides us with the means to persevere through the pain and overcome that resistance; all we have to do is ask for and receive it. Once we do, we begin the journey to our authentic selves.

Such a journey is not only desirable but imperative. Jesus himself took such action before he began his public life when he fasted and prayed in the desert. It was a necessary daily discipline to take time away and be alone with his Father. Even

Jesus, divine though also human, had to confront temptations and fears; we must do the same. In following our Lord's example, we find that the journey of self-discovery is not a self-indulgent act but one of love, toward ourselves and our Creator. It is an act of humility in which we come face-to-face with the ugly truths and weaknesses in our lives and give them over to God. It is a fruitful action, empowering us with the confidence and vision to carry out the wonderful life plan that God has given to us. Our deep dive is *meant* to disturb us, to turn us away from stagnation toward growth.

I believe this is why Jesus insisted on disturbing people with his teachings and actions: "Do not think that I have come to bring peace to the earth; I have not come to bring peace, but a sword" (Mt 10:34). He wanted to shake people out of complacency and provincial thinking. He desired that each person grow spiritually, meeting their true selves and thus meeting him. He knew that pride prevented people from grasping the truth. Time and again he wrangled with the religious leaders over aspects of the Law and how it should be observed. Jesus wanted to lead them beyond the outer performance tailored for an audience to a deeper observance in the secrecy of their hearts—from pride to humility.

While the parables seem simple enough, Jesus meant for them to be provocative, employing the power of storytelling and common illustrations to foment questions about who we are, what we truly desire, what love of God and neighbor means, what forgiveness entails, and what it costs to follow him. Those of us who "hear" will then search within ourselves for the meaning. He knew that many would not understand: "They may indeed look, but not perceive, and may indeed listen, but not understand" (Mk 4:12).

We see him stirring up the crowds by declaring that one had to eat his flesh and drink his blood to be his follower; several disciples left him that day. Jesus' predictions of his suffering and death created confusion and inner turmoil for his disciples. Peter took him to task over it and was subsequently rebuked: "You are setting your mind not on divine things but on human things" (Mt 16:23). Jesus' cruel death was almost too much to bear; Thomas was so traumatized that he refused to believe that the Lord had risen without physical proof.

Jesus called on everyone he met to do what he did on a daily basis: search within. He asks the same of us. The gospels share several occasions when he dealt with conflict, fear, temptation, and anguish. During his forty days in the desert as described in Matthew 4:1–11, Jesus was tempted by the devil, first by material want (by using his divine power to create bread out of stones, thus breaking his self-imposed fast), second by a desire to prove God's love for him (by throwing himself off from the top of the Temple), and third by the lure of worldly wealth and splendor (if he pledged his allegiance to Satan).[2] In each case Jesus as man remains true and united to his divine nature by rejecting these temptations. While there is no clear description of a struggle, it doesn't take much to imagine that, hungry and alone, Jesus may have experienced inner conflict, perhaps even fear. He was being disturbed to the core of his being. In persevering through his struggle, Jesus emerged with a clear sense of his mission. He knew who he was, and what he had to do.

In the Garden of Gethsemane the conflict was deeper. Here Jesus confronted the reality of the death he was about to suffer; it was the point of no return, and he resisted. In chapter 14, St. Mark described Jesus' anguish as he threw himself to the ground, perhaps tempted to the point of despair, waves of fear engulfing him. Reflecting on his experience, I was reminded of my dear mother, succumbing to despair because she was unable to find a way of connecting with anyone who could help her. Jesus, in praying to his Father, using the intimate Aramaic term *Abba,* which translates to "Daddy," was able to ward off despair. Remembering the look in my mother's eyes, I wondered if Jesus also had that same look of stark terror, even for a brief moment, as he prayed.

Jesus questioned his fate; it was a moment suspended in time. Like any of us, he did not wish to die; he did not seek out suffering.[3] He knew, however, that it was his destiny. As in the desert, he was tempted to give in to the human inclination to run away from suffering: "Remove this cup from me." But, strengthened by his union with his Father in prayer, Jesus acquiesced: "Yet, not what I want, but what you want" (Mk 14:36). Father Martin writes that "Jesus displays a more confident attitude after his prayer . . . no longer the man collapsed in barely restrained grief on the ground; he is in command."[4] The perfect union of his humanity and divinity provided Jesus with the strength to face the unimaginable. He was to emerge from suffering and death, and rise to new life. Because of this, we too are now capable of a union of humanity and divinity (though imperfect due to sin) through the reception of his Holy Spirit within us when we are baptized. We can reinforce that unity again and again by receiving his Body and Blood in the Eucharist. We need never go spiritually hungry or thirsty. By acknowledging God's presence within us, we can be empowered by the river of grace.

When we allow ourselves to be disturbed, we open ourselves up to the possibilities of the Holy Spirit; for the first time we may be able to sense God within. It can be the beginning of that change within, known as conversion, a movement from indifference and stagnation to intention and growth. It is a creative process that transforms, turning us away from the false god of the self to the living and true God. It calls for an honest and often painful accounting of who and what we are. It also leads to the exhilarating adventure of discovering who God means for each of us to be.

Sometimes we are nudged out of complacency, inspired by something we've experienced. Other times we are jolted as in the case of losing a loved one or facing our own mortality. In every case, we lose something significant, something we dearly love. But we also gain. Rich had to give up his old life in a parish he loved and endure misunderstanding in order to realize his true self as a deacon. I had to lose my parents and my singing voice so that I could conquer my fear, gain back my creative self, and realize my vocation as a writer.

We cannot avoid loss or suffering. We cannot avoid fear. We can choose to withdraw or flee, or we can run straight into the pain, a potential and roaring river of grace that can lead to discovery, growth, healing, and transformation. We can interpret suffering as meaningless and the causes as random, or we can look deeper to see its life-changing power.

In my faith formation I was taught to link my own pain and suffering to that of Jesus because his agony was personal and redemptive. We can trust that he understands our afflictions, having lived through many of them himself. Through his death and resurrection he grants us the hope that we too can rise again from our losses and pain. Life, death, and resurrection define the cycle of life that we witness again and again in ourselves and those around us. I think of Jackie enduring her inner-ear disease while greeting each new day with the resolve to make it count. I reflect on Reg living with the many repercussions of her near death after the birth of her child, struggling through her limitations and making a real mark on her world. And I smile thinking of my sister, emerging from her grief and resurrecting her long-dormant passion for painting.

When our human spirit unites with God's grace within, anything is possible. Taking that first small step into the river of grace, we enter into a state of prayer that is ongoing whether we are aware of it or not. It may not be a prayer made up of words, but simply a sense of immersion into something greater than ourselves. If we have become disciplined in daily spiritual practices such as reading the Bible, meditating, examining our consciences, offering petitions and prayers of thanksgiving, or journaling while reading a spiritual book, we can consciously tap into that steady stream of prayer. It is this continuous engagement that opens our eyes to what God sees. It is what equips us to take that deep dive and perceive what lies inside of the soul. In the river of grace we learn the beauty of humility, recognizing and understanding our pain and brokenness and uniting it all with the One who heals and makes us whole. We become filled to overflowing with the fruits of such prayer, our bounty then naturally pouring out to those around us. With our hearts and minds filled with God, we can step out boldly into the world and be as Christ to everyone we meet.

My earliest encounters with the river of grace came in the midst of losing my parents. The force of the river kept me afloat through the turbulence of their illnesses and gave me the strength to endure the pain. Immersed in the river, I was able to show them my love despite my fears and inhibitions. Grace helped me to persevere in my continuous prayers for their souls. It gave me the wisdom and humility to reach out to family and friends for their prayer support and consolation. I attribute grace to bringing Fr. Giggi to us when we needed him most, ministering to my father at our home and then my mother at the hospital. He offered absolution for their sins, opening the path for their salvation. Grace opened my eyes to signs around me, reassuring me that my prayers for them were not and would not be in vain; this comforted me in my grief.

In this same river I discovered gratitude, that sweet recognition and appreciation for gifts bestowed on me for no other reason than the pure love of the Giver. The river produced a wellspring of inner joy and wonder through the simple actions of reading and writing. It gave me peace and harmony with my husband, acquired through trips together in the kayak and beyond. Grace restored my singing voice through emotional and physical healing. It awoke my slumbering creative life by deepening my thirst for learning and spiritual insight, daring me into a journey of self-discovery. Grace exposed the tyranny of fear and provided small invitations to step out as a means of conquering that fear. Absorbed in the river of grace, I am confident in who I am, living the life I was meant to live. For the first time I can embrace the beautiful treasure of my existence as a child of God, given to me out of his mysterious and unfathomable love.

Imagine yourself as a child of God, loved beyond understanding. Think about the life he desires for you, the treasures he has planted within you beneath the still waters of the river. Do you believe that his love is enough for you to rise above your pain, your losses, your grief? Do you believe you can be made whole again?

Take your first step into the river of grace and ponder God's love for you as described in this song, "In His Eyes" by Mindy Jostyn and Jacob Brackman:

> In His eyes, you're a fire that never goes out
> A light on the top of a hill
> In His eyes you're a poet, a painter, a prophet
> With a mission of love to fulfill
> Outside there's a world so enchantingly strange
> A maze of illusion and lies

But there's never a story that ever could change
The glory of you in His eyes

In His eyes you're a radiant vision of beauty
A gemstone cut one of a kind
You're fine as a diamond, deep as a ruby
Rare as a jade in His mind
No need to believe all you may have been told
No need to live in disguise
You're brighter than silver, purer than gold
A pearl beyond price in His eyes . . .

In His eyes, you're a fire that never goes out
A light on the top of a hill
You're a rose in the forest, a prelude from Bach
A triumph of heavenly skill
Outside there's a world that keeps breaking your heart
And tearing your dreams down to size
But guiding you homeward, piercing the dark
Is the lovelight that shines in His eyes
Now and forever, that light never dies
You're dearly beloved in His eyes.[5]

Flow Lesson 17

In His Eyes

Materials needed: pen or pencil and paper, computer or tablet, a bible, an image or icon of Jesus

Before beginning this exercise, take a few moments to be still and sense the presence of God with you. Ask the Holy Spirit to guide you through this activity and reveal what he wants you to know.

Open your bible to Psalm 139 and read verses 1–18 out loud. Do you believe that God is your Father, your *Abba* ("Daddy")? Do you believe you are a special and unique creation, fashioned by his hand? Recall an adult in your life (mother, father, relative, or friend) to whom you are especially close:

- How do you feel when you are with this person? Do you trust this person and believe what he or she says? Why? What has this person done to earn your trust?

- How would that person describe you? If you don't know, consider asking him or her.

- Think of that person when you think of God as Daddy. Have you ever thought of God in such a personal and intimate way? Why or why not?

- Do you find it easier to think of God the Father as Daddy or of Jesus as your closest friend? Why or why not?

Now listen to Mindy Jostyn sing a portion of "In His Eyes" (visit beasone.org, click on "Resources" tab and then "Flow Lesson 17" to find this video). You can read along, beginning with "In His eyes you're a radiant vision of beauty . . ."

Listen to the song a second time, either gazing on your image or icon of Jesus or closing your eyes and imagining Jesus looking at you straight in the eye and singing this to you. Do you feel the sentiments in this song are true for you? Why or why not?

Take a piece of paper and fold it in half. On the left-hand side, list all the things about yourself that you like. Then slowly and deliberately thank God for each item on your list.

On the right-hand side, list those things about yourself that you either don't like or feel are a burden to you. Write down any feelings these things bring up.

Compare your lists: Which one is longer? Why do you think that list is longer? What does it say about you?

Remembering that God makes no mistakes and that all things have an ultimate purpose for good, tell God honestly how you feel, and offer these things to him that you don't like about yourself, asking him to use them for his glory and your benefit. Do not be alarmed or put off if you have negative feelings because God knows us through and through; share with him as honestly as you can. Be prepared that this could be a hard prayer to offer; you may need to repeat this prayer over time.

Ready to Say Yes?

The river of grace is within each of us, waiting to do its creative work of transforming our lives. When the Renaissance artist Michelangelo began his sculptures, he saw not a slab of stone waiting to be formed into beautiful art, but beautiful art hidden within the slab that needed to be released and shown to the world. "In every block of marble I see a statue as plain as though it stood before me, shaped and perfect in attitude and action. I have only to hew away the rough walls that imprison the lovely apparition to reveal it to the other eyes as mine."[6]

That same magnificence lies within each of us. When we respond with a yes to that first small invitation, recognizing the potential for movement and growth within the throes of loss and grief, our journey begins.

As I have been so empowered, enriched, and blessed by my journey, I pray that yours will be the same.

Questions for Reflection

1. Do you sense any invitations from God to try something new? What is he asking you to do? Do these invitations strike you as unusual? Do they require you to step outside of your comfort zone? How do you feel about that?

2. Does the envy of someone else's skills prevent you from seeing your own strengths? Describe those skills you desire. Are there strengths of your own that could accomplish something good? List those strengths, thanking God for them and asking him to use them for his glory.

3. How has your love for others helped you to overcome fear? What specific actions did you take or can you take to fight through fear for the love of another?

4. Have you experienced a sudden and profound change in your life that you did not expect? Describe the circumstances. How did this change make you feel? Have you been changed as a result, and how? Or have you experienced a change in your life that has caused pushback or misunderstanding from people you love? What happened and how did you respond? Was the change in your life worth what you experienced? Why or why not?

5. How do you feel about taking a journey of self-discovery? Are you concerned that doing so is an act of self-centeredness? Following the example of Jesus, how can learning more about yourself be an act of love, toward yourself and others?

6. Think of yourself as a slab of stone—what magnificence and beauty lie within, waiting to be brought forth? What steps can you take to start chiseling away at that slab of stone?

Visit beasone.org, click on the "Resources" tab and then "Flow Lessons" for additional activities to facilitate a deeper exploration of the concepts of this chapter. Videos, music, and examples are supplied to help you with these exercises.

Acknowledgments

Writing this book was both a dream come true and a pure gift from God. It would never have happened without the help and support of numerous friends, colleagues, fellow parishioners, and especially my family.

First, to my muses, Louisa May Alcott and Joni Mitchell: thank you for teaching me to love words. Thank you for inspiring me and giving me insight into my creative life. And to St. Teresa of Avila and St. Thérèse of Lisieux, the "reluctant" writers: thank you for your intercession and inspiration.

I am grateful to songwriter Matthew Baute for sharing his song "River of Grace" with me back when we first got the kayak; this song helped me to make that connection between the river and God's grace.

I am indebted to my colleagues on the Commission for Women of the Diocese of Worcester, Massachusetts. My experiences with you have stretched me far beyond what I could have imagined. You entrusted me with the writing of our monthly column for the *Catholic Free Press*, following in the footsteps of pioneer members Mary Donovan and Margaret Diggins. In writing articles highlighting the speakers at our 2013 Gather Us In women's conference, I was privileged to write about the delightful Sr. Bridget Haase, O.S.U. It was Sr. Bridget who connected me with Lil Copan, then an acquisitions editor for Ave Maria Press; the rest, as they say, is history. I am profoundly grateful to Sr. Bridget for believing in me and bolstering my efforts with her encouragement and prayers.

Lil Copan's appreciation of my vision and her expert and patient direction helped this neophyte writer to craft her first book and, because of that, to experience the adventure of a life-time. Bob Hamma's gracious yet firm guidance helped to perfect the vision and crafting of this book, making it something of which I am immensely proud. I can't thank Lisa Hendey enough for being a lifeline when I most needed it. Her willingness to take time out of her busy schedule to read my early efforts, offer her reassurances, and pray for me provided needed strength to get through the rough patches.

I could not have written this book without my faithful readers and their fearless appraisals: Reg Cram, Jackie Silverstein, and my sister, Christine Houde. Your encouragement along with notes, suggestions, and honest critique shaped this book in so many ways. I will forever cherish the many hours of meaningful conversation we shared as a result.

I am so grateful to my writing teacher, Amy Belding Brown, whose wisdom, skill, encouragement, and gentle cri-tique guided me through the early stages of writing. To blogger extraordinaire and author Jeff Goins I am indebted for helping me to declare, "I am a writer!" I want to thank Michael Hyatt for his informative blog and materials on writing; it was his guide on how to write a book proposal that led me in my presentation to Ave Maria Press.

To my blogging communities at *Louisa May Alcott Is My Passion* and *Be As One*: thank you for sticking with me, engag-ing in thought-provoking conversation, and encouraging me in my writing vocation. I never would have discovered my love of research nor my writing vocation without your help.

To Fr. Steven LaBaire and Monsignor Michael Foley: thank you for your spiritual guidance and your examples of service and holiness. Your encouragement and sage advice helped me to step out and take a risk with this book. Thank you to my parish community of St. Luke the Evangelist in Westborough, Massachusetts, especially to Gloria Josephs for all your little "invitations," and to Julie Basque for introducing me to Jackie Silverstein and for instilling in me through your example a devotion to the Blessed Mother and an understanding of grief. To Deacon Dave McDowell: my thanks for reading through the manuscript, ensuring that I made no serious theological errors. Your years of friendship, support, and gentle challenges helped me to find and embrace my inner mystic.

To my parents, Herb and Deb Hoyle: I thank you for giving me lessons of self-sacrificing love and devotion to family, love of silence and music, my introduction to the Catholic Church, and a passion for learning, reading, and the natural world. Thank you for helping me to learn about the power and importance of empathy toward others. To the Bailey and Tedoldi families, thank you for teaching me the power of hospitality and the wonderful, creative ways you show your love to me.

To my children, Stephen and Meredith: my love and pride for you knows no bounds. I continue to revel in your growth as the caring and committed adults that you are. You never fail to teach and to move me.

And to my husband of thirty-eight years, Rich: your love sustains me and fills me with gratitude and wonder at the gift of our marriage from God. Your no-nonsense approach to decision-making and time management, plus your generosity in giving me the space and time I needed, made the writing of this book possible.

Notes

1. Discovering the Flow of Grace

1. Maria Faustina Kowalska, *Diary: Divine Mercy in My Soul* (Stockbridge, MA: Marian Press, 2005), 224, 524.

2. Vinny Flynn, *7 Secrets of the Eucharist* (San Francisco: Ignatius Press, 2006), 1.

3. E. L. Doctorow, "The Art of Fiction No. 94," *Writers at Work: The Paris Review Interviews, Eighth Series* (New York: Penguin Books, 1988).

2. Allowing Grace to Grow

1. Daniel B. Hinshaw, *Suffering and the Nature of Healing* (Yonkers, NY: St Vladimir's Seminary Press, 2013), 16.

2. James Martin, S.J., *Jesus: A Pilgrimage* (New York: HarperOne, 2014), 224.

3. Thérèse de Lisieux, *The Story of a Soul (L'Histoire d'une Âme): The Autobiography of St. Thérèse of Lisieux with Additional Writings and Sayings of St. Thérèse*, trans. Thomas Nimmo Taylor, Kindle version (Amazon Digital Services, Inc., March 24, 2011), chapter 9.

4. Mother Teresa, *Come Be My Light: The Private Writings of the "Saint of Calcutta,"* ed. Brian Kolodiejchuk (New York: Image, 2009).

5. Quotations on the Eucharist, *Children of Hope*, http://
www.childrenofhope.org/childrenadore/quotes.htm.

6. John F. Russell, "St. Thérèse and Her Little Way," *Society
of the Little Flower*, http://www.littleflower.org/abouttherese/
learn/stThereseLittle.asp.

7. Thérèse de Lisieux, *Story of a Soul: The Autobiography
of St. Thérèse of Lisieux*, 3rd ed., trans. John Clarke (ICS Publications, 1996), 72.

3. Flowing with the Current

1. "Tedy Bruschi," *Wikipedia*, http://en.wikipedia.org/
wiki/Tedy_Bruschi.

2. Neil Norman, "Julie Andrews: Depression, Pain and
Why I'm Now Able to Make My Comeback," *Express*, May 8,
2010, http://www.express.co.uk/expressyourself/173883/Julie-
Andrews-Depression-pain-and-why-I-m-now-able-to-make-
my-comeback.

3. Demetrios Trakatellis, "Seeing and Believing: The
Thomas Incident (John 20:24–29)," *Greek Orthodox Archdiocese
of America*, 1998, http://www.goarch.org/ourfaith/ourfaith8173.

4. Patrick Reidy, C.S.C., Homily, from the broadcast
of the Sunday Mass at the Basilica of the Sacred Heart, Notre
Dame, CatholicTV, April 27, 2014.

5. Trakatellis, "Seeing and Believing."

6. Flynn, *7 Secrets of the Eucharist*, 15.

7. Ibid., 14.

8. M. Regina Cram, *Do Bad Guys Wear Socks? Living the
Gospel in Everyday Life* (CreateSpace Independent Publishing
Platform, 2012), 135.

9. Ibid., 101.

10. Ibid.

11. Ibid., 138.

12. Hinshaw, *Suffering and the Nature of Healing*, 52.

13. Colleen M. Story, "Can Stress Cause Acid Reflux?" *Healthline*, June 30, 2012, http://www.healthline.com/health/gerd/stress.

4. Exploring New Tributaries

1. Louisa May Alcott, *Little Women* (Brooklyn: A. L. Burt Company, 1911), 360.

2. Ibid., 357.

3. Gloria Delamar, *Louisa May Alcott and "Little Women": Biography, Critique, Publications, Poems, Songs and Contemporary Relevance* (iUniverse, 2001), 16.

4. Louisa May Alcott, *Work: A Story of Experience* (New York: Penguin, 1994), 320.

5. Anatole Broyard, "Towards a Literature of Illness," *Sorrow's Company: Great Writers on Loss and Grief*, ed. Henry DeWitt (Boston Beacon Press, 2001), 201.

6. Lisieux, *Story of a Soul*, 71–72.

7. Joyce Rupp, *Praying Our Goodbyes: A Spiritual Companion Through Life's Losses and Sorrows* (Notre Dame, IN: Ave Maria Press, 2012), 48.

8. Jacques Gauvin, *Wine and Wineskins*, November 2010, http://jacquesgauvin.com/website/speeches/wineskins.html.

9. Rupp, *Praying Our Goodbyes*, 46–47.

5. Diving Deep

1. Martin, *Jesus: A Pilgrimage*, 276.

2. Ibid., 283.

3. Vinita Hampton Wright, *The Soul Tells a Story: Engaging Creativity with Spirituality in the Writing Life* (Downers Grove, IL: IVP Books, 2005), 12–13.

4. Ibid., 125–126.

5. Ibid., 16.

6. Ibid., 25.

7. Ibid., 16.

8. Ibid., 83.

6. Testing New Waters

1. Amy Welborn, "Suscipe, the Radical Prayer," *Ignatian Spirituality*, excerpt from *The Words We Pray*, http://www.ignatianspirituality.com/ignatian-prayer/prayers-by-st-ignatius-and-others/suscipe-the-radical-prayer/.

2. Martin, *Jesus: A Pilgrimage*, 104.

3. Ibid., 330.

4. Ibid., 336.

5. Mindy Jostyn and Jacob Brackman, "In His Eyes," music recording, Say No More Music (BMI) and Maya Productions (ASCAP), 1998, http://www.mindyjostyn.com/lyrics_in_his_eyes.shtml.

6. Jaletta Albright Desmond, "Life Lessons from Michelangelo's 'David,'" *DavidsonNews.net*, August 5, 2011, http://davidsonnews.net/blog/2011/08/05/life-lessons-from-michelangelos-david/.

Bibliography

Alcott, Louisa May. *Little Women*. New York: A. L. Burt Company, 1911.

————. *Work: A Story of Experience*. New York: Penguin, 1994.

Cram, M. Regina. *Do Bad Guys Wear Socks? Living the Gospel in Everyday Life*. CreateSpace Independent Publishing Platform, 2012.

Delamar, Gloria. *Louisa May Alcott and "Little Women": Biography, Critique, Publications, Poems, Songs, and Contemporary Relevance*. iUniverse, 2001.

Desmond, Jaletta Albright. "Life Lessons from Michelangelo's 'David'." *DavidsonNews.net*. August 5, 2011. http://davidsonnews.net/blog/2011/08/05/life-lessons-from-michelangelos-david/.

Dewitt, Henry, ed. *Great Writers on Loss and Grief*. Boston: Beacon Press, 2001.

Flynn, Vinny. *7 Secrets of the Eucharist*. San Francisco: Ignatius Press, 2006.

Gauvin, Jacques. *Wine and Wineskins*. November 2010. http://jacquesgauvin.com/website/speeches/wineskins.html.

Hinshaw, Daniel B. *Suffering and the Nature of Healing*. Yonkers, NY: St Vladimir's Seminary Press, 2013.

Jostyn, Mindy, and Jacob Brackman. "In His Eyes." Music Recording. Say No More Music (BMI) and Maya Productions (ASCAP), 1998. http://www.mindyjostyn. com/lyrics_in_his_eyes.shtml.

Kowalska, Maria Faustina. *Diary: Divine Mercy in My Soul.* Stockbridge, MA: Marian Press, 1987.

Lisieux, Thérèse de. *The Story of a Soul (L'Histoire d'une Âme): The Autobiography of St. Thérèse of Lisieux with Additional Writings and Sayings of St. Thérèse.* Translated and illustrated by Thomas Nimmo Taylor. Amazon Digital Services, Inc., March 24, 2011.

————. *Story of a Soul: The Autobiography of St. Thérèse of Lisieux.* 3rd ed. Translated by John Clarke. Washington DC: ICS Publications, 1996.

Martin, James. *Jesus: A Pilgrimage.* New York: HarperOne, March 11, 2014.

Norman, Neil. "Julie Andrews: Depression, Pain and Why I'm Now Able to Make My Comeback." *Express.* May 8, 2010. http://www.express.co.uk/expressyourself/173883/Julie-Andrews-Depression-pain-and-why-I-m-now-able-to-make-my-comeback.

Quotations on the Eucharist. *Children of Hope.* http://www. childrenofhope.org/childrenadore/quotes.htm.

Rupp, Joyce. *Praying Our Goodbyes: A Spiritual Companion Through Life's Losses and Sorrows.* Notre Dame, IN: Ave Maria Press, 2012.

Russell, John F. "St. Thérèse and Her Little Way." *Society of the Little Flower.* http://www.littleflower.org/therese/reflections/st-therese-and-her-little-way/.

"Tedy Bruschi." *Wikipedia.* http://en.wikipedia.org/wiki/
      Tedy_Bruschi.

Trakatellis, Demetrios. "Seeing and Believing: The Thomas
      Incident (John 20:24-29)." *Greek Orthodox Archdio-
      cese of America.* 1998. http://www.goarch.org/ourfaith/
      ourfaith8173.

Welborn, Amy. "Suscipe, the Radical Prayer."
      Ignatian Spirituality. Excerpt from *The Words
      We Pray.* http://www.ignatianspirituality.com/
      ignatian-prayer/prayers-by-st-ignatius-and-others/
      suscipe-the-radical-prayer/.

Wright, Vinita Hampton. *The Soul Tells a Story: Engaging Cre-
      ativity with Spirituality in the Writing Life.* Downers
      Grove, IL: IVP Books, 2005.

BACKGROUND READING

Bondi, Renee, and Nancy Curtis. *The Last Dance but Not the Last
      Song.* Ada, MI: Baker Publishing Group, 2002.

Mother Teresa. *Come Be My Light: The Private Writings of the
      "Saint of Calcutta."* Edited by Brian Kolodiejchuk. New
      York: Image, 2009.

Potok, Chaim. *The Gift of Asher Lev.* New York: Fawcett Books,
      1997.

———. *My Name is Asher Lev.* New York: Anchor, 2003.

Sabiner, Karen, ed. *The Empty Nest: 31 Parents Tell the Truth
      About Relationships, Love, and Freedom After the Kids Fly
      the Coop.* New York: Hachette Books, 2008.

S usan Bailey is a blogger, musician, and speaker who fre-
quently contributes to *CatholicMom.com* and the Asso-
ciation of Catholic Women Bloggers. Her work has also
appeared on *Catholic.net*, and *Catholic Online*. Bailey blogs at
Be As One and *Louisa May Alcott Is My Passion*. She also writes a
monthly column for *The Catholic Free Press* called "Be As One."

Bailey, who works as a marketing/advertising assistant,
was a member of the Commission for Women of the Diocese of
Worcester, Massachusetts, where she served as chair and secretary
and helped organize the biennial Gather Us In conference. A
professional musician and graphic artist, Bailey released three
CDs, performed on EWTN and CatholicTV and at World
Youth Day in 2002. She worked as a cantor for fifteen years. She
earned a bachelor's degree in elementary education (US History
and music) from Bridgewater State University.

She and her husband, Rich, have two grown children and
live in North Grafton, Massachusetts.

AVE MARIA PRESS

Founded in 1865, Ave Maria Press,
a ministry of the Congregation of
Holy Cross, is a Catholic publishing
company that serves the spiritual and
formative needs of the Church and its
schools, institutions, and ministers;
Christian individuals and families; and
others seeking spiritual nourishment.

For a complete listing of titles from

Ave Maria Press

Sorin Books

Forest of Peace

Christian Classics

visit www.avemariapress.com

AVE MARIA PRESS
Notre Dame, IN
A Ministry of the United States Province of Holy Cross